Applying NCTE/IRA Standards in Classroom Journalism Projects

NCTE Editorial Board: Jacqueline Bryant, Kermit Campbell, Willie Mae Crews, Colleen Fairbanks, Andrea Lunsford, Gerald R. Oglan, Jackie Swensson, Gail Wood, Zarina M. Hock, Chair, ex officio, Kent Williamson, ex officio, Peter Feely, ex officio

Applying NCTE/IRA Standards in Classroom Journalism Projects

Activities and Scenarios

Candace Perkins Bowen
Kent State University

Susan Hathaway Tantillo
Wheeling (Illinois) High School

NCTE National Council of Teachers of English
1111 W. Kenyon Road, Urbana, Illinois 61801-1096

JEA Journalism Education Association
Kansas State University, 103 Kedzie Hall
Manhattan, KS 66506-1505

Royalties from this book will be donated to the Journalism Education Association.

Staff Editor: Tom Tiller
Interior Design: Doug Burnett
Cover Design: Diana C. Coe
Cover Image ©Arthur Tilley/Getty Images

NCTE Stock Number: 32707-3050

JEA Stock Number: 639

©2002 by the National Council of Teachers of English.

All rights reserved. No part of this publication may be reproduced or transmitted in any form or by any means, electronic or mechanical, including photocopy, or any information storage and retrieval system, without permission from the copyright holder. Printed in the United States of America.

It is the policy of NCTE in its journals and other publications to provide a forum for the open discussion of ideas concerning the content and the teaching of English and the language arts. Publicity accorded to any particular point of view does not imply endorsement by the Executive Committee, the Board of Directors, or the membership at large, except in announcements of policy, where such endorsement is clearly specified.

Although every attempt is made to ensure accuracy at the time of publication, NCTE cannot guarantee that all published addresses for electronic mail or Web sites are current.

Library of Congress Cataloging-in-Publication Data

Bowen, Candace Perkins, 1947–
    Applying NCTE/IRA standards in classroom journalism projects : activities and scenarios / Candace Perkins Bowen, Susan Hathaway Tantillo.
        p. cm.
Includes bibliographical references.
    ISBN 0-8141-3270-7 (pbk.)
  1. Journalism—Study and teaching (Secondary)—United States. I. Tantillo, Susan Hathaway, 1946– II. Title.
    PN4788 .B69 2002

2002012087

Contents

Acknowledgments vii

Introduction ix

Standard 1 1

Comparing Publications 1
    Susan Hathaway Tantillo
Vignette: Comparing Media Coverage 6
    Susan Hathaway Tantillo
Vignette: Mining University Archives for Today's Information 9
    John Bowen

Standard 2 16

Using Literature in a Journalism Class 16
    Carol Lange

Standard 3 22

A Dozen Media Comparison Activities 22
    Candace Perkins Bowen and Susan Hathaway Tantillo
Organizing a Story 24
    Susan Hathaway Tantillo

Standard 4 26

Illustrating Passive Voice with Actions 26
    H. L. Hall
Using Research to Create a "Newspaper" 28
    Candace Perkins Bowen
Vignette: Adapting to a Varied Audience 34
    Michele Dunaway

Standard 5 37

Comparing an Editorial and a News Story 37
    Susan Hathaway Tantillo
Vignette: Reporting on the Witch's Trial 39
    Candace Perkins Bowen

Standard 6 42

Vignette: Collaborating on an Editorial 42
    Lisa O. Greeves

Standard 7 — 51
Vignette: Applying "Real-World" Research — 51
  Donna M. Spisso

Standard 8 — 55
Gathering Internet Sources — 55
  Richard P. Johns
Vignette: Getting a Student Newspaper Online — 57
  Candace Perkins Bowen

Standard 9 — 64
Vignette: Collaborating with Videoconferencing — 64
  Candace Perkins Bowen

Standard 10 — 67
Vignette: Bringing What You Can — 68
  Candace Perkins Bowen
Reaching Out into the Community — 68
  Susan Hathaway Tantillo
Checking Out the Commercial Press — 70
  Susan Hathaway Tantillo
Vignette: *Expresión Juvenil,* a Spanish Newspaper That Started as a Class Project — 72
  Eugenia Sarmiento Lotero

Standard 11 — 75
Vignette: Understanding a Web Audience — 75
  Candace Perkins Bowen with Christine Kaldahl
Vignette: Reaching Across the Ocean — 78
  Candace Perkins Bowen

Standard 12 — 81
Vignette: Mentoring Future Journalists — 81
  Candace Perkins Bowen
Vignette: Reporting on the Community — 84
  Candace Perkins Bowen

Conclusion — 91

Authors — 93

Contributors — 95

Acknowledgments

Special thanks to Journalism Education Association (JEA) board members John Bowen, Lakewood, Ohio; Michele Dunaway, Ballwin, Missouri; H. L. Hall, Hendersonville, Tennessee, and Carol Lange, Reston, Virginia; and to JEA members Lisa Greeves, Vienna, Virginia; Dick Johns, Iowa City, Iowa; and Donna Spisso, Dhaka, Bangladesh, for the vignettes they wrote.

Thanks also to those who contributed background and class materials and allowed the authors to interview them: Rick Ayers, Iliana Montauk, and Megan Greenwell, Berkeley, California; Shirley Yaskin and Jamie Kleinerman, Miami, Florida; Matt Leifer and Bridget Rubenking, Lakewood, Ohio; Kirin Kalia, Amsterdam, Netherlands; Deb Buttleman Malcolm, Davenport, Iowa; Christine Kaldahl, Omaha, Nebraska; Eugenia Sarmiento Lotero, Denver, Colorado; Dianne Smith and David Rosen, Hastings, Texas; Leeanne Alsept, Dennison, Ohio; Jill Martin and Joe Paris, Kent, Ohio.

And, finally, thanks to Howard Spanogle, Asheville, North Carolina, for his Elizabethan Newspaper Unit idea that I enjoyed teaching for so many years I almost believed it was mine. He and other journalism teachers across the nation have helped each other design assignments, solve technical dilemmas, fight censorship, and generally survive in schools where they are often the only ones teaching journalism. This book is dedicated to those "Lone Rangers," the one or two teachers at each school who give students the background to produce a newspaper, yearbook, Web site, or television or radio program. They already know how valuable these lessons are for their students. Perhaps this book will help them convince others.

—Candace Perkins Bowen

Introduction

What Does Journalism Teach?

Sarah was excited when she left her third-period journalism class. She had just completed a story about her school district's proposed budget and formatted it on a page for her school newsmagazine. It hadn't been easy.

Her idea to write the story first came when she heard her mother's friend complaining about the increase in taxes she might expect if the school levy passed. The next day, her biology teacher warned the class that the frog experiment everyone enjoyed in sophomore science might be cancelled this year because no budget would cover it. Sarah and the others in her class were disappointed. When she walked into the journalism room, her editor was looking for story ideas for the next issue.

"What's happening that could affect our readers?" he asked. "We want something more than who was Homecoming Queen and when the French Club meets." Sarah wondered if the tax levy might be a story. It certainly sounded like it would make a difference to the biology students. Could it mean no more field trips for senior English classes to see the live production of *A Christmas Carol?* And she had heard that the district might finally get a newer edition of the junior history books, one that included the Persian Gulf War. Would that purchase be postponed again? Sarah knew she never read about topics like tax levies when they ran in the community paper. The articles were always full of numbers and words she didn't understand, like "mills" and "apportionment." But maybe she could find a way to show how those numbers and words made a difference in her life and those of her classmates. She added "tax levy" to the story list and signed her name beside it.

The story took Sarah almost a month to complete. First, she checked her local newspaper's archives on the Internet to read background. Since she didn't understand what all the articles meant, she met with her economics teacher after school so he could help her define some terms and put the information in simpler language that both she and her readers would understand. She also learned how to calculate what her school would get from a tax increase and what percentage of their budgets administrators would have to cut if the levy failed. She had a question for her government teacher, too, about how many voters needed to support the levy for it to pass and what would happen next if they said no. Next she set up interviews with the principal and the president of the school board, developed a preliminary list of questions for them, conducted her interviews while taking careful notes and asking follow-up questions when she didn't understand, and transcribed the parts she knew she might use in her story. She found a few other expert sources, including her biology teacher and the department heads of English and social studies, all of whom would be affected. Then she talked to some students, too, to get their perspectives.

At first, she thought she wanted to write an editorial about the levy, but her editor and publications adviser convinced her to do a news story so that readers would understand all the facts and sides of the controversy, and *then* she could also write a commentary, presenting her viewpoint. It meant more writing, two stories instead of one, but it seemed like a fair way to present the information. For both pieces, she wrote a preliminary draft, received some coaching from both her editor and her adviser to help her spot areas that might not be clear to readers, revised, ran it past them and some other staff members again, caught a few mechanical errors, then polished the final product.

Still she wasn't finished. Sarah and her editor both understood the figures she used in the story, but they wanted to make the information as clear as possible to readers. What if she created an informational graphic from some of them? Sarah didn't consider herself an artist, but she did know how to use a drawing program on the computer. After a little assistance from the staff's graphics editor, she put together an attractive box of information that showed at a glance how much the school's budget would shrink and in what probable areas if the levy didn't pass. At last, the story, along with a suggested headline and Sarah's informational graphic, went to her page editor. The two of them used a desktop publishing program to package the pieces together for page six of the next newsmagazine.

Clearly, Sarah learned a great deal from this—she used skills typical of English class to gather information and draft and polish a story; of civics or economics class to understand taxation and voter input; of mathematics class to figure percentages; of art class to design a layout and create a graphic that conveys information; and of technology class to word-process and desktop-publish it all. Given the right story, the list of skills Sarah uses and the knowledge she gains in completing a journalism project covers almost every aspect of her education.

Journalism's Connection with the Twelve NCTE/IRA Standards

Journalism teachers have long recognized their courses and the often extracurricular media they produce as excellent ways to teach a vast range of high school, junior high/middle school, and even elementary school content. Their courses support teaching standards for various curricula and indeed could—and probably should—be allowed to support an entire set of standards uniquely their own. However, because that is not an option in most states, and because journalism courses are most often part of English departments, with instructors who also have English or integrated language arts education background, it is only natural to create a book to strengthen this link.

Standards for the English Language Arts, published in 1996 by the National Council of Teachers of English and the International Reading Association, represents four years of work by thousands of educators. Their shared purpose, according to the introduction, is "to ensure that all students are knowledgeable and proficient users of language so that they may succeed in school, participate in our democracy as informed citizens, find challenging and rewarding work, appreciate and contribute to our culture, and pursue their own goals and interests as independent learners throughout their lives" (Farstrup and Myers, 1996, vii).

The members of the Journalism Education Association (JEA) share those goals. JEA continually seeks to provide its membership—composed primarily of high school and junior high/middle school teachers of journalism, mass media, broadcast, and related courses—with resources and educational opportunities so they can be more effective in working with their students. One area of concern for them is professional development, and one way to help them grow is to assist them in understanding and assessing current educational trends and how those trends relate to scholastic journalism. The use of standards for curriculum, including the language arts, is just such a trend.

Taken one at a time, the NCTE/IRA standards clearly parallel what JEA encourages its members to provide in their classrooms. Each standard can be easily fulfilled in any journalism course, whether its focus is gathering information from a wide variety of sources, presenting ideas to different audiences and for different purposes, or appreciating the diversity that characterizes communication. A high school journalism class might support all of these standards. A junior high English class might focus on one or two through a single unit. Even elementary teachers can utilize journalism in relatively simple, media-related assignments with their classes.

Taken as a whole, the NCTE/IRA standards and JEA's goals show mutual concern for using a wide range of texts and materials to help students understand themselves and others, now and in the future. In addition, both groups value the importance of educational opportunities for all students to ensure that they are informed citizens who can contribute to society.

The Purpose of This Book

With these goals in mind, the following chapters illustrate how journalism class projects and journalism-oriented assignments not only fulfill the twelve NCTE/IRA standards but also offer exciting, hands-on options at various teaching levels. Some apply best to beginning journalism courses, often titled Journalism 1 or Journalistic Writing. Others are more appropriate for a publications or broadcast staff, either as a course or as a focused learning session for an extracurricular activity. Some work as a unit in a secondary school English class, while others are aimed at elementary or junior high/middle school students. Although the following vignettes and discussions each correspond to a selected standard, it is also clear that each overlaps with and helps support other standards. Some segments of the book depict actual situations in specific classrooms, while others represent a lesson typical of journalism classes across the nation, and one vignette in Chapter 7 even goes beyond the United States.

Because of our commitment—like the commitment of every educator—to help students become better thinkers, better communicators, and, as a result, better citizens, members of JEA invite all teachers to bring the real world into their classrooms. To do this, teachers can use the vignettes and approaches offered here as a starting point.

The Twelve Standards

Standard 1

Students read a wide range of print and nonprint texts to build an understanding of texts, of themselves, and of the cultures of the United States and the world; to acquire new information; to respond to the needs and demands of society and the workplace; and for personal fulfillment. Among these texts are fiction and nonfiction, classic and contemporary works.

Standard 2

Students read a wide range of literature from many periods in many genres to build an understanding of the many dimensions (e.g., philosophical, ethical, aesthetic) of human experience.

Standard 3

Students apply a wide range of strategies to comprehend, interpret, evaluate, and appreciate texts. They draw on their prior experience, their interactions with other readers and writers, their knowledge of word meaning and of other texts, their word identification strategies, and their understanding of textual features (e.g., sound-letter correspondence, sentence structure, context, graphics).

Standard 4

Students adjust their use of spoken, written, and visual language (e.g., conventions, style, vocabulary) to communicate effectively with a variety of audiences and for different purposes.

Standard 5

Students employ a wide range of strategies as they write and use different writing process elements appropriately to communicate with different audiences for a variety of purposes.

Standard 6

Students apply knowledge of language structure, language conventions (e.g., spelling and punctuation), media techniques, figurative language, and genre to create, critique, and discuss print and nonprint texts.

Standard 7

Students conduct research on issues and interests by generating ideas and questions, and by posing problems. They gather, evaluate, and synthesize data from a variety of sources (e.g., print and nonprint texts, artifacts, people) to communicate their discoveries in ways that suit their purpose and audience.

Standard 8

Students use a variety of technological and informational resources (e.g., libraries, databases, computer networks, video) to gather and synthesize information and to create and communicate knowledge.

Standard 9

Students develop an understanding of and respect for diversity in language use, patterns, and dialects across cultures, ethnic groups, geographic regions, and social roles.

Standard 10

Students whose first language is not English make use of their first language to develop competency in the English language arts and to develop understanding of content across the curriculum.

Standard 11

Students participate as knowledgeable, reflective, creative, and critical members of a variety of literacy communities.

Standard 12

Students use spoken, written, and visual language to accomplish their own purposes (e.g., for learning, enjoyment, persuasion, and the exchange of information).

Work Cited

Farstrup, Alan E., and Miles Myers. 1996. "Introduction." Pp. vii–viii in *Standards for the English Language Arts*. Urbana, Ill.: National Council of Teachers of English, and Newark, Del.: International Reading Association.

Standard 1

Students read a wide range of print and nonprint texts to build an understanding of texts, of themselves, and of the cultures of the United States and the world; to acquire new information; to respond to the needs and demands of society and the workplace; and for personal fulfillment. Among these texts are fiction and nonfiction, classic and contemporary works.

Using Journalism

In working with models and sources of information, students read, view, and listen to a wide range of media in their journalism, English, and language arts classes. Local, national, and international newspapers serve to show them differences in writing styles and graphic presentations, from their weekly community papers to the staid *Wall Street Journal* to the garish tabloids of Great Britain. In addition, students in journalism classes view television to assess its ability to balance its entertainment and informational roles. Magazines reflect interests and concerns of their readers, often in very selective niche markets, and they provide students with a look at both fiction and nonfiction for varied audiences. Spanning all the media is advertising, which is a lesson in persuasion and often, in today's society, a necessary means of delivering messages to mass audiences. And mass media offer a glimpse of various readers and viewers, display diverse cultures and regions, and generally provide information about the world around us. *The Veronis, Suhler & Associates Communications Industry Forecast, 1997–2001* estimates that each person spends approximately one-third of his or her time sleeping, a little over a quarter (28 percent) awake but not using media, and nearly 39 percent exposed to video, audio, online, or print media. Understanding what such sources contain is vital. This is definitely one way students gain information, interact with society, and achieve personal fulfillment.

Comparing Publications

By Susan Hathaway Tantillo

"Mrs. T, why don't we look at the *National Enquirer* as an example of journalism? Those journalists make tons of money, I think, and my mom even subscribes to it and reads it more than she reads a daily newspaper. How much money could somebody make working for the *National Enquirer* anyway?"

Questions like these are a good starting point for a comparative study of types of newspapers and newsmagazines. Students can draw conclusions not only about the differences and similarities between supermarket tabloids, professional daily newspapers, and high school student newspapers, but also about the basic purposes of these different media—information, influence, entertainment, service.

In one approach to this type of comparative study, the class divides into groups of three, and each group chooses a supermarket tabloid, a professional daily, and one or more high school student newspapers to examine. The teacher starts by asking each group to construct a series of sentences they can defend as being true of one or more of the publications in their group. For example, they might conclude that all are sold for a specific price, supermarket tabloids are the most expensive of the three, all use photographs to attract readers, and all can be obtained by subscription. Once they have made their initial observations, each group shares its list with the class. Group members must be able to show examples to back up what they say.

Once we have processed the observations from all groups, each group receives a list of statements and must decide whether each statement is true for only one of the examples in front of them, two of the examples, or all three. Once again, students must be able to demonstrate with specific reference to the sample publications why they came to the conclusions they reached. Once each group finishes the list of observations, the teacher combines smaller groups so they can resolve any differences in their answers. Once they have debated and resolved their answers, small groups report out to the large group and resolve any remaining differences.

In this way, students draw their own conclusions about different media purposes and how those purposes are carried out. Weekly professional newsmagazines and weekly professional newspapers could also be added to the mix.

Here is the worksheet students receive after the groups of three have made their own initial observations about similarities and differences between their samples:

Newspaper Comparison Project

Journalistic Writing 1

S. Tantillo

Note: Each person in the group should fill out his or her own sheet to keep. In addition, you will need one sheet from the group to turn in.

Names of Group Members: _____
_____
_____
_____
_____

For this project, our group used the following publications:

Supermarket tabloid: _____
Chicago-area professional daily: _____
High school newspapers: _____
_____
_____

After a thorough review of the publications you have listed above, decide as a group the best answer for each of the statements below. Be prepared to defend your answer by showing an example or using logic as proof.

   A. Supermarket tabloids only
   B. Chicago-area professional newspapers only
   C. High school newspapers only, as represented by the *Spokesman* and others
   D. Both A and B
   E. Both A and C
   F. Both B and C
   G. All three

   ___ 1. Is distributed free as its usual means of reaching readers.
   ___ 2. Charges advertisers a set fee.

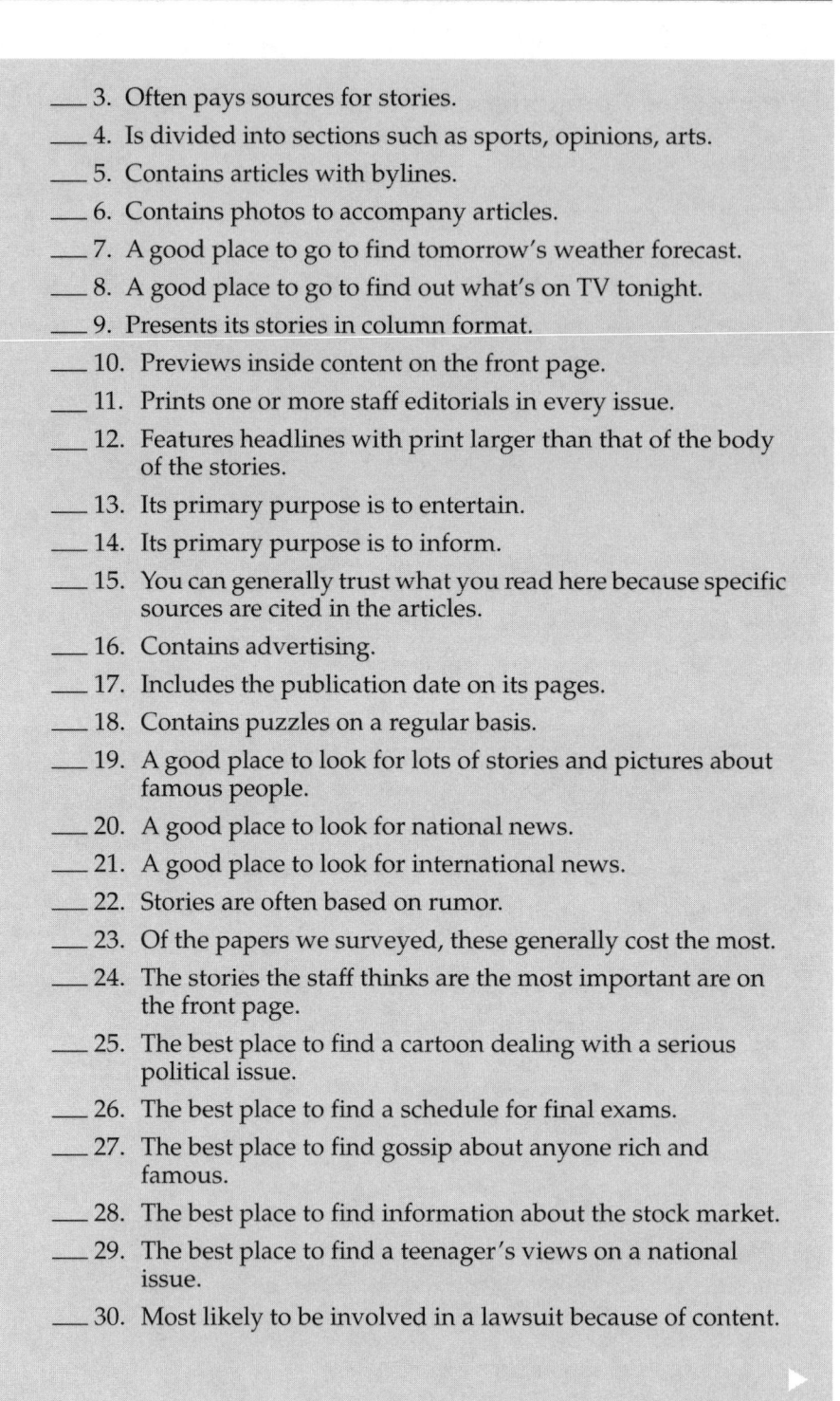

___ 3. Often pays sources for stories.
___ 4. Is divided into sections such as sports, opinions, arts.
___ 5. Contains articles with bylines.
___ 6. Contains photos to accompany articles.
___ 7. A good place to go to find tomorrow's weather forecast.
___ 8. A good place to go to find out what's on TV tonight.
___ 9. Presents its stories in column format.
___ 10. Previews inside content on the front page.
___ 11. Prints one or more staff editorials in every issue.
___ 12. Features headlines with print larger than that of the body of the stories.
___ 13. Its primary purpose is to entertain.
___ 14. Its primary purpose is to inform.
___ 15. You can generally trust what you read here because specific sources are cited in the articles.
___ 16. Contains advertising.
___ 17. Includes the publication date on its pages.
___ 18. Contains puzzles on a regular basis.
___ 19. A good place to look for lots of stories and pictures about famous people.
___ 20. A good place to look for national news.
___ 21. A good place to look for international news.
___ 22. Stories are often based on rumor.
___ 23. Of the papers we surveyed, these generally cost the most.
___ 24. The stories the staff thinks are the most important are on the front page.
___ 25. The best place to find a cartoon dealing with a serious political issue.
___ 26. The best place to find a schedule for final exams.
___ 27. The best place to find gossip about anyone rich and famous.
___ 28. The best place to find information about the stock market.
___ 29. The best place to find a teenager's views on a national issue.
___ 30. Most likely to be involved in a lawsuit because of content.

Standard 1

___ 31. Its stories are mostly based on fact, but some contain the writers' or staff's opinions.

___ 32. Is an example of a broadsheet.

___ 33. Contains classified advertising.

___ 34. Is supported by taxpayer money.

___ 35. The staff is made up entirely of volunteers.

___ 36. Contains mostly weird stories.

___ 37. Has the price of an issue printed on the cover.

___ 38. Least likely place to find a four-color photo.

___ 39. Readers are likely to depend on a detailed index to help them find stories.

___ 40. Best place to find student and faculty quotes about the start of the school year.

___ 41. Features a front page consisting only of headlines, no stories.

___ 42. Most likely to contain a story about a "cure" for a rare disease.

In which publication would you be most likely to find each of the following headlines? Use the space below each headline to explain your reasoning.

___ 43–44. "Investigators' top secret report: Kidnap attempt killed Diana & Dodi"

___ 45–46. "Chaos from Kremlin to Wall Street"

___ 47–48. "No vote yet as District 214 puts science labs under the microscope"

___ 49–50. "Diana: Shocking new evidence about her death"

___ 51–52. "Feds focus probe on NU football"

___ 53–54. "Airport limits gain mayor's backing"

___ 55–56. "Ferrer, Dzien, Malin win conference titles"

___ 57–58. "Three WHS musicians place in top IMEA positions, qualify for other top honors"

___ 59–60. "Della collapses after losing 21 pounds"

Finally, on the back of this sheet, come up with at least five other statements you can make about newspapers, similar to the first forty-two, and use the same letters (A through G) to indicate which type(s) of newspaper they apply to. In each case, explain in writing why you chose the answer you did. Be sure to include these on your own sheet as well as on the master sheet for your group.

Vignette: Comparing Media Coverage

By Susan Hathaway Tantillo

When a major political figure in the throes of a presidential campaign, like George W. Bush, makes national news for what he thinks is a private comment heard only by his running mate, a prime teachable moment occurs. The old cliché—truth is stranger than fiction—is proven true again.

In the fall of 2000, presidential candidate Bush inadvertently created the perfect opportunity for teachers everywhere to use the daily newspaper to talk about audience and appropriateness, both on the part of the public speaker and on the part of the person covering the speaker.

Here are the facts: Presidential candidate George W. Bush visited Naperville, Illinois, on Monday, September 4. While standing with his running mate Dick Cheney behind what Bush thought was a closed microphone, Bush commented to Cheney about *New York Times* journalist Adam Clymer. However, what Bush thought was a private comment to Cheney was anything but private. The open microphone picked it up, allowing everyone attending the Labor Day rally to hear it.

On the following day, September 5, Chicago-area newspapers chose different approaches in covering the event as a news story, as shown by these summaries:

- The *Daily Herald*, a major suburban broadsheet daily, ran its story under the headline "Bush puts foot in his mouth with remark." Without using the term by which Bush referred to Clymer, the story's opening two paragraphs stress the incident. Paragraph two quotes Bush as saying to Cheney, "There's Adam Clymer, a major league (expletive deleted) from *The New York Times*." In fact, the *Daily Herald* never mentioned the word Bush used, either in news stories or in follow-up coverage by a columnist or editorial writers.

- The *Chicago Sun-Times*, a Chicago tabloid which carries a banner proclaiming itself as the "Midwest's Best-Read Newspaper," ran its story on page one under the headline "Bad Word: Bush gets caught." The one-sentence lead paragraph refers to a Chicago rally for Al Gore, mentions a Cheney campaign stunt, and finally alludes to Bush's using an obscenity in Naperville. The story continues for another two and a half paragraphs on page one and then jumps to page four before the end of the fourth paragraph. On page four, readers immediately find out Bush actually said Clymer was a "major league asshole."

- The *Chicago Tribune*, a Chicago broadsheet, ran its story under the headline "Candidate blitz greets holiday / In Naperville, Bush touts straight talk as Democrats' wives attend Navy Pier rally." Unlike the previous two examples, the *Tribune's* lead paragraph does not directly mention Bush's comment to Cheney. In fact, the story never directly quotes the comment at all—with or without the actual word. Paragraph two tells that Bush, in talking to Cheney, referred to a *New York Times* reporter using an expletive. It also says Cheney agreed. Thirteen paragraphs later in the story, the reporters return to the quote idea, calling Bush's comment to Cheney "the most noteworthy comment" of the Naperville campaign stop. In the next paragraph, the reporters write, "he [Bush] turned to Cheney and used a vulgar term to describe *Times* reporter Adam Clymer." Like the *Daily Herald,* the *Chicago Tribune* never used Bush's word, not in the news story and not in a columnist's follow-up coverage.

By Wednesday, September 6, the Reuters news service had a story available about the event and how newspapers covered it. The first three paragraphs of that story follow (copyright 2000 by Reuters; reprinted with permission):

NEW YORK — The news Tuesday was "the word." The *Washington Post*, *Los Angeles Times* and *USA Today* printed the word, and the *New York Times* said only it was "an obscenity." The *Washington Times* used another term for the body part that could be seen as equally objectionable.

The word had major U.S. newspapers doing cartwheels after Republican presidential candidate George W. Bush referred to a reporter that way in Naperville when he believed the microphone was turned off.

The story goes on to quote Dr. Joyce Brothers and others about how society adapts to changes in language, with additional examples of words which have become commonplace because they are used more often.

On that same day, Chicago-area columnists were using the event as though nothing else had happened in the last twenty-four hours. One interesting point for discussion with students is the difference in how columnists write about a topic and how news reporters write about the same topic. Consider these different approaches:

- John Kass, *Chicago Tribune* columnist, wrote under the headline "Bush has a word for jerk, but few feel it's fit to print." Without reprinting Bush's exact word, Kass pokes fun at the *New York Times* itself and then summarizes media reaction to Bush's remark. He concludes that most media didn't print "the word."

- Jack Mabley, *Daily Herald* columnist, wrote under the headline "George W.'s faux pas hurts nice guy image." Without reprinting Bush's actual remark, Mabley hints heavily at it by calling it a "seven-letter word describing a body part beginning with A." He concludes that, while anyone who is provoked may often use such words, presidential candidates should have better sense than to do so where a microphone can pick them up.

- Richard Roeper, *Chicago Sun-Times* columnist, wrote under the headline "He had the Kiss, but can Gore top the Dis?" In his column, Roeper advises Gore to capitalize on Bush's disrespectful remark in Naperville the previous day. He does not repeat Bush's comment, referring to it as "an offhand remark." But he does tie it ironically to Bush's Naperville campaign speech, which followed the remark and in which Bush said, "It's time to elect people who say what they mean and mean what they say."

Also on Wednesday, September 6, the *Chicago Sun-Times* ran an editorial cartoon by Jack Higgins that was inspired by the event, and the *Daily Herald* devoted its lead staff editorial to the slip, characterizing it as one of several Bush had made in the last week. Under the headline "For Bush, a week of errors," the editorial points out that the expletive Bush used to describe Clymer contradicts his promise "to bring greater civility to public discourse."

By Thursday, September 7, the *Chicago Sun-Times* devoted about one-third of its letters space to those related to the Bush gaffe.

Teachers can access a collection of articles such as these at a public library or at newspaper Web sites. If copied and pasted electronically into a teacher's word-processing files on the day of publication, they can be used later without the fee for accessing archived material on the original Web site.

A teacher might show students one news article at a time and ask them what they would do—print "the word" or use a euphemism for it. Have students list reasons for their decision. This could result in a lively classroom discussion or debate. Then ask them to decide from their parents' point of view, or their younger brother's or sister's. Do they have different opinions depending on the audience?

You might also show students a columnist's approach compared to a news reporter's approach and ask them to list the differences and similarities. This can lead to a class discussion about tone. Which approach do they think provides the better picture of what happened? Which gives them more "food for thought"? Or, after reading what more than one columnist has to say, students might be asked which approach they like better and why.

Other comparisons can be done between reviews of the same book, movie, TV show, or CD, or between competing national newsmagazines—e.g., *Time*, *Newsweek*, and *U.S. News & World Report*—to study how they cover the same story. Ask students to bring examples of their own for class discussion. Of course, they won't always be able to find such an impressive example involving a major political candidate!

Vignette: Mining University Archives for Today's Information

By John Bowen

When the newsmagazine staff at Lakewood (Ohio) High School realized that the anniversary of a noteworthy event was taking place less than an hour's drive away, they decided to explore how to cover it. May 4, 2000, was the thirtieth anniversary of the death of four students at Kent State University during an antiwar protest on campus. Of course the Lakewood students could write about what would be happening on campus to commemorate the event, or simply write the history, but they wanted to report more than that. They thought their readers would be interested in the impact that May 4, 1970, had made on activism and what it still means for students today.

Matt Leifer, editor in chief, summed up their goal: "We were a group of people who cared a lot about a cause—freedom of expression. One thing we wanted to show was the wrongs that smothered that expression back then. We were also interested in seeing just how much of an impact those students (at Kent State) had in Ohio, the U.S., the world."

The first step was a February trip to the Kent campus fifty miles away. There, Matt and four other editors invaded unfamiliar territory—the university archives—to gather background and perspective information about the shooting of thirteen students on campus thirty years ago. These archives came in the form of more than a hundred boxes, each containing folders of handwritten notes, photographs, published articles, movie footage, and audiotapes. Some items, such as poetry and letters of support, came from as far away as Russia.

At first the students were daunted by all they saw. They didn't know where to begin, although each had outlined his or her primary area of reporting. As they settled into their work, they began to skim articles, then to read more thoroughly. They shared, telling others if they found something that might be useful or could lead to other interviews or research.

"I was surprised to see letters of support for the students from Scotland and France and many other universities in those files. That helped show how far it reached," Matt said.

At one point, another researcher in the archives noticed what the students were doing and questioned them about it. He was with the Learning Channel and became one of a number of valued sources for their final publication.

What the students found in the archives validated information they had obtained from other sources and, in some cases, led to story angles and sources they had not considered. One student found more detailed and localized information about the Students for a Democratic Society (SDS)—notes and memos, some even handwritten, from SDS officers on campus in the late '60s. This information led to sources across the country that the student journalist could interview, some of whom had been at Kent State before and during the shootings, including one woman who had helped found the organization in Kent and who now lives in Oregon.

Another student, Bridget Rubenking, immersed herself in background about one wounded student, Alan Canfora, and set up a time to meet with him in person. "I would have felt incredibly stupid interviewing him if I didn't know exactly what I was talking about," Bridget said. "While he was a little rehearsed and had definitely made this the story of his life, I was still determined to find out something new."

Knowing Canfora's strong biases, Bridget was also inclined to double-check some of the "facts" he gave her. For instance, *Campus*

Unrest: The Report of the President's Commission on Campus Unrest supported what Canfora said about the weapons he saw. She also checked sources that offered a different view of Canfora's assertion that the government, not the students, burned the ROTC building. (See sidebar story below.)

Students made three trips to the archives, even though originally they had thought they would need only one. They quickly saw the importance of document-based research using a variety of sources. Exploring the archives helped them develop a more thorough understanding of the era and find more sources for their articles. The closing three pages of the publication even included telegrams and letters—some as digitally scanned reproductions in the original handwriting—to Kent State students and administrators from as far away as Europe.

"Without the information from the archives, we still would have had stories, but they wouldn't have been as complete as they were," Matt said. "We also wouldn't have had the added touches like the letters that appear at the end of the issue."

Their twenty-eight-page special publication about the thirtieth anniversary of the deaths of four college students at Kent State demonstrated historical and, more important, personal perspective that would not have been possible without students' use of the archives.

Days of Protest Lead to Lifelong Pursuit

By Bridget Rubenking, Lakewood (Ohio) High School

Alan Canfora uses the words "martyrs," "executions," "conspiracies," and "militant" quite often in describing his experience on May 4 and his feelings about it.

Canfora, shot in the wrist May 4, along with 12 others, four of whom died, has remained politically active from his days in the Young Democrats and Students for a Democratic Society to his now public quest to make sure people do not forget about the Kent State tragedy. Canfora also works to register voters.

Canfora was on the commons as part of the rallies and said he was an active protester the whole weekend. He said that is why he was shot.

Photos show him waving a black flag May 4, shortly before the National Guard began to shoot. "It was a symbol of anarchy, despair and anger," he said. "At that period of time, a lot of people my age felt alienated from the government."

Many students and Vietnam War protesters were alienated because both Democrats and Republicans supported the war, Canfora said.

Canfora said he, along with other protesters, was not a real philosophical anarchist but knew the risks they were taking.

"I was shot within the first one or two seconds of gunfire," Canfora said. "I'm convinced I was a target because I was one of the more vocal protesters."

He said during the next 11 or 12 seconds his main concern was to stay behind a tree to stay alive. "I knew the tree was absorbing some bullets. It was saving my life," he said.

Canfora said he looked to the right and saw his roommate, Tom Grace, wounded.

"He was shot in the foot. It blew his boot right off. He was sitting up to look at it, so I said, 'Stay down! Stay down!' And he did."

The Guard had M-1 rifles, some shotguns, .45 caliber pistols, but most of the shots were fired from the M-1's, Canfora said.

According to *Campus Unrest, The Report of the President's Commission on Campus Unrest*, the majority of the shots were from M-1 rifles, though Donald S. MacKenzie's wound was ruled not severe enough to be from an M-1 or .45 caliber pistol. Several doctors agreed he was shot with a smaller caliber weapon, possibly a carbine. No proof was found, though, of any other weapons or snipers.

Canfora said his wound was painful and bloody.

"It was quite horrifying, surreal. I knew I had to get to the hospital myself," Canfora said. So, after the shooting stopped and people were helping Grace, he tried to go to the hospital.

"I saw Jeffrey Miller, whom I had been introduced to a few months earlier. I didn't know he was dead," Canfora said.

"I just kept running through the parking lot."

Canfora was able to stop a car and get a ride to the hospital where he was then treated.

"I insisted I be released. Even though they wanted to keep me in the hospital, I told them I was leaving," he said. "I was concerned I might be arrested at the hospital, so I had to get out."

Canfora said he then ran into his sister, girlfriend, roommate and friends outside the hospital, and they went to his house.

"We were all very angry. We knew we had witnessed a massacre," he said. "I was a victim, and more importantly, I was an eyewitness."

Canfora said he was later arrested "as part of the political repression in Kent and consequently put on probation for three years and not allowed in Kent or on the campus itself."

"I call that my period of exile," he said. "Those were some crazy years down at Kent, with government agents and other things."

Canfora finished his bachelor's degree from the Stark County Kent campus in 1972. In 1980 he received his master's degree in library science.

Since then, Canfora said he has tried to educate students and others about the events of May 4 as an important part of American history that cannot be forgotten for fear of something like it happening again.

He said he will occasionally get a letter from a student who is doing a school assignment or is just curious. He said he always replies.

Canfora's involvement does not begin or end there, however. He was involved in political organizations on campus, as well as the events of the three days before the shootings, and has remained active with students groups about May 4 since.

"When I first arrived at Kent in September of '68, Tom [Grace] and I joined the Young Democrats." Canfora said he was active with that group in its efforts to support Hubert Humphrey against Nixon.

About a month after that, he quit Young Democrats because they were "not effective" and not doing much.

Canfora said he then joined the SDS, which was "far more determined and passionate." The SDS had speakers, Canfora said, and they listened to different people. He went with the SDS to Washington, DC in January 1969, to protest Nixon's inauguration and was there during the "dramatic and militant" actions that occurred.

He said the experience was very powerful, and the returning students took that feeling back with them.

In April 1969, the group was thrown off the Kent State campus, and its leaders, along with 70 others, were arrested for their "militant actions," Canfora said.

"We had deep, sincere, legitimate concerns," Canfora said.

It was schoolmates and childhood friends going to war, Canfora said. "It was deep concerns for our friends who were dying every day and concern about the killing of Asian people as well."

Canfora said he was in downtown Kent Friday night May 1 and around the ROTC building Saturday night, as students tried to set it on fire.

Friday, May 1, a large group of students gathered downtown, blocked traffic and broke some windows. The following night, one of the ROTC buildings was burned down.

"It's really most significant we led the crowd down the street," he said. "I'd like to point out, without revealing my own actions, I was in the thick of it and one of the main participants."

It was the same people involved Saturday as Friday, and the ROTC building was not burned when the students were chased away.

"The building was burned to the ground after we were sent away from the area," he said.

"I think it's a good possibility the building was burned by the government or police agents trying to make an excuse for the governor to call on the National Guard."

Canfora said he has no proof of this, but others saw it.

According to the presidential commission's report, "Only a dozen or so persons appeared to have made efforts to set the building afire."

The report mentioned no other parties responsible for the fire other than students who created a large group around the building and prevented firefighters from reaching the fire.

Canfora said the main cause of the unrest on campus was student anger at the Vietnam War and, most recently, Nixon's April 30 announcement of the invasion of Cambodia.

"Vietnam went on so long because our generation was kind of naïve," Canfora said.

"We trusted the government too long. Even though young people are more aware today, it could still happen again. If people don't remember the lessons of Vietnam and Kent State, we could see another war or another massacre like Kent."

Canfora said in part because of May 4, Nixon was forced to pull troops out of Cambodia within the next few weeks, and that started the overall task of bringing the soldiers home.

"The martyrs" of Kent State, Canfora said, along with the nationwide students' strike following the shootings, resulted in change.

"The shootings had a big impact on politics, the government and the military," Canfora said. "We didn't choose our place in history."

Works Cited

The Report of the President's Commission on Campus Unrest. 1970. Washington: GPO.

The Veronis, Suhler & Associates Communications Industry Forecast, 1997–2001. 1997. New York: Veronis, Suhler & Associates.

Standard 2

Students read a wide range of literature from many periods in many genres to build an understanding of the many dimensions (e.g., philosophical, ethical, aesthetic) of human experience.

Using Journalism

Although literature does not appear at first to be a staple of journalism classes, many programs have incorporated it effectively. For instance, when requirements for all California English classes in the 1980s included literature/fiction, a committee representing the Southern California Journalism Education Association (SCJEA) and the Journalism Education Association of Northern California (JEANC) put together course outlines utilizing authors from Mark Twain to Ernest Hemingway, many of them, incidentally, former journalists. Literature is also apparent in a growing number of classes across the country that are part of the intensive journalistic writing program begun with support from the Dow Jones Newspaper Fund. These classes use journalism models instead of more traditional expository pieces to prepare students to pass the Advanced Placement English Composition test. Today, ten years after the program was launched, journalism students who took this intensive journalism writing course consistently score higher on the composition test from the College Board than do those who took a traditional AP English class. The most recent scores show that those with journalism background earned 3 or higher on the five-point scale 72 percent of the time, while the English students passed at a 65.1 percent rate. This course material, available to teachers through workshops at such sites as Indiana University, Marquette University, and the Freedom Forum, includes much that relates literature to journalism.

Using Literature in a Journalism Class

By Carol Lange

> I often feel drawn to the Hudson River, and I have spent a lot of time through the years poking around the part of it that flows past the city. I never get tired of looking at it; it hypnotizes me. I like to look at it in midsummer, when it is warm and dirty and drowsy, and I like to look at it in January, when it is carrying ice. I like to look at it when it is stirred up, when a northeast wind is

> blowing and a strong tide is running—a new-moon tide or a full-moon tide—and I like to look at it slack. . . . I knew that every spring a few sturgeon still come in from the sea and go up the river to spawn, as hundreds of thousands of them once did, and I had heard tugboatmen talk about them, but this was the first one I had ever seen. It was six or seven feet long, a big, full-grown sturgeon. It rose twice, and cleared the water both times, and I plainly saw its bristly snout and its shiny eyes and its white belly and its glistening, greenish-yellow, bony-plated, crocodilian back and sides, and it was a spooky sight.

Using journalistic basics, we could ask students to discuss who wrote this passage, what it is about, where it takes place, when it takes place, why the author begins his work about rivermen with this paragraph, and how the opening of this work affects them as readers.

"The Rivermen" was written by Joseph Mitchell, a New York newspaper feature writer who spent the last years of his career at the *New Yorker*. Considered one of the great literary journalists, Mitchell presents observation and research, blends fact with personal emotion, and utilizes strong descriptive writing and sentence structure—and we have read only the first paragraph.

A study of this paragraph allows the journalism student to discuss several literary devices, to analyze order of details, and to examine the impact of an opening paragraph upon the reader. When is the first person effective and appropriate, and when is it not? What does one know about the first-person narrator by the end of the first paragraph? Is there a phrase or word choice that is particularly appealing?

Literary journalists produce excellent models. Journalism teachers can use the works of such literary journalists as John McPhee, Brent Staples, Jane Kramer, David Quammen, and of course Mitchell to introduce students to a wide array of topics. These writers' essays and books clearly illustrate the interdisciplinary nature of journalism and the need for journalists to have curiosity.

If journalism teachers are not persuaded that literary journalism meets the definition of "literature," they might go in another direction to bring literature into their journalism classes. For example, many high school newspaper staffs select the most opinionated member of the journalism course to be a columnist or review writer; however, while his or her opinion pieces may stimulate discussion among some students, this is no way to develop the student's writing skills or to educate journalism students and their readers to be better consumers. Instead, a teacher might consider adding a unit of study on review writing.

Movie and music reviews have become expected components of an entertainment section, and book reviews should be there as well. In fact, the writing of book reviews, the reading of varied literature, and journalism instruction form a natural alliance. "Literature instruction that starts with students' responses to texts adds personal relevance as well as depth and breadth to their understanding of those texts," according to the NCTE Positions and Guidelines document "Defining and Defending Instructional Methods" (see section 4, "The Teaching and Learning of Literature," at http://www.ncte.org/positions/defend.shtml).

Students need instruction in the art of review writing, and they need to read works with content, context, and presentation that enable a strong review. Journalism teachers should collect well-written models of book reviews. These may be found in their local newspapers or online at sites such as the following: *New York Times* (http://www.nytimes.com/pages/books/index.html), *Los Angeles Times* (http://www.calendarlive.com/top/1,1419,L-LATimes-Books-X!Front,00.html), and *Washington Post* (http://www.washingtonpost.com/wp-dyn/style/books/). These sites provide many book reviews as well as meet-the-author features, first chapters, and online book discussions.

For basic instruction in review writing, visit the Commentary and Columns section of the "Only a Matter of Opinion?" Web site at http://library.thinkquest.org/50084. This site is a project of ThinkQuest for Tomorrow's Teachers. The work found on the site was developed for use in a hybrid course encompassing Advanced Placement English language and composition/intensive journalistic writing, but it can easily be used in any English or journalism course. The site includes instruction in writing columns and book reviews, as well as a student model and discussion of how to use models in the classroom.

According to the NCTE Positions and Guidelines document cited above, "The student/teacher community of interpreters develops knowledge by talking and writing about their reactions to a wide variety of texts." To accomplish this, try one of the following approaches to review writing.

Book Club Approach

Five students each month nominate five "must-read" books. Divide the class into five groups, with a different work being read by each group. After reading, students meet in groups to discuss the work. Give students some possible focuses for their conversation, e.g., strengths and weaknesses of the plot, character development and theme, best part of the work, worst use of language, or most memorable passage. Would they recommend the work to another student?

A Thematic Approach

Each month, the book review could focus on a different theme. What might interest your students? Are there anniversaries in your community or significant events to which you and your students might relate? For example, would your students enjoy poet Rita Dove's meditations found in *On the Bus with Rosa Parks,* or *Rosa Parks: My Story* by Rosa Parks and James Haskins? Here are three themes to get you started:

Books That Have Made the New York Times *Bestseller List*

Many Americans bought these books. What do your students think of them? You might select works that appeared in the past, those that remained on the list for many weeks, or those on this month's list. *Tuesdays with Morrie,* appearing on the list for more than a year, isn't "just a book for girls." Sports fans might know author Mitch Albom for his excellent sports coverage in the *Detroit Free Press* or one of his collections. *Tuesdays with Morrie* also has the potential for comparison with the made-for-television movie *Oprah Winfrey Presents: Tuesdays with Morrie.*

Books That Have Been Censored or Challenged

In 2000, J. K. Rowling and her Harry Potter works were at the top of the challenged list. If you wish to keep the focus on challenged children's works, the list could include *Little Red Riding Hood* by Jacob and Wilhelm Grimm, *James and the Giant Peach* by Roald Dahl, *Bridge to Terabithia* by Katherine Paterson, *Blubber* by Judy Blume, and *A Wrinkle in Time* by Madeleine L'Engle.

Challenged and banned books for older readers might include one of the most challenged works, *Adventures of Huckleberry Finn* by Mark Twain. Also providing perspectives on the cultures of the United States would be *Of Mice and Men* by John Steinbeck, *I Know Why the Caged Bird Sings* by Maya Angelou, *The Call of the Wild* by Jack London, and *The Right Stuff* by Tom Wolfe. Those who relish irony would enjoy *Fahrenheit 451* by Ray Bradbury.

Visit the NCTE Anti-Censorship site at http://www.ncte.org/censorship/ for various resources including the NCTE position statement on students' right to read, guidelines for dealing with censorship of nonprint materials, and information about rationales for challenged books.

Books about Nature

As the weather warms and thoughts turn to outdoor activities, suggest a book to take along on the hike or picnic. These could cover a range of fiction and nonfiction. *Prodigal Summer* by Barbara Kingsolver places the reader amidst the flora and fauna in southern Appalachia. If your students read *Walden*, add *Pilgrim at Tinker Creek* to this list. Do students see Annie Dillard as a contemporary Thoreau? Pair *Into Thin Air* by Jon Krakauer with *On Top of the World: Climbing the World's 14 Highest Mountains* by Richard Sale and John Cleare.

Two works highly praised in the nature genre are Rachel Carson's *Silent Spring* and Lewis Thomas's *The Lives of a Cell*. Students might be asked to read one of these, then find a contemporary work with which to compare and contrast it.

An International Approach

Review the English edition of books that were originally written in another language, or books written in English by international authors. If your school has a language immersion program or has many students whose first language is other than English, you might have them read and review books as written in another language.

Read Across America

If your school is involved in the National Education Association–sponsored Read Across America program, your newspaper might review works by Dr. Seuss or other works that your students could read to students in a nearby elementary school. Or if your staff is working with younger students to develop a newspaper with a book review column, visit the American Library Association's best books site (www.ala.org/rusa/bestbooks.html) for possible selections. Don't neglect students' favorites from childhood.

Book reviews get students to read, to evaluate, and to write. Reviews are persuasive pieces that require an understanding of audience and purpose. And, as Dr. Seuss promised, oh, the places you'll go once the first page is read and turned to the next.

NCTE/IRA Standards Addressed in a Book Review Writing Assignment

The numbering used below is that of the official NCTE/IRA standards.

   1. Students read a wide range of print and nonprint texts to build an understanding of texts, of themselves, and of the cultures

of the United States and the world; to acquire new information; to respond to the needs and demands of society and the workplace; and for personal fulfillment. Among these texts are fiction and nonfiction, classic and contemporary works.

2. Students read a wide range of literature from many periods in many genres to build an understanding of the many dimensions (e.g., philosophical, ethical, aesthetic) of human experience.

3. Students apply a wide range of strategies to comprehend, interpret, evaluate, and appreciate texts. They draw on their prior experience, their interactions with other readers and writers, their knowledge of word meaning and of other texts, their word identification strategies, and their understanding of textual features (e.g., sound-letter correspondence, sentence structure, context, graphics).

4. Students adjust their use of spoken, written, and visual language (e.g., conventions, style, vocabulary) to communicate effectively with a variety of audiences and for different purposes.

5. Students employ a wide range of strategies as they write and use different writing process elements appropriately to communicate with different audiences for a variety of purposes.

6. Students apply knowledge of language structure, language conventions (e.g., spelling and punctuation), media techniques, figurative language, and genre to create, critique, and discuss print and nonprint texts.

11. Students participate as knowledgeable, reflective, creative, and critical members of a variety of literacy communities.

Standard 3

Students apply a wide range of strategies to comprehend, interpret, evaluate, and appreciate texts. They draw on their prior experience, their interactions with other readers and writers, their knowledge of word meaning and of other texts, their word identification strategies, and their understanding of textual features (e.g., sound-letter correspondence, sentence structure, context, graphics).

Using Journalism

Messages from mass media bombard us daily, from the morning newspaper, to the talk show on the car radio en route to school, to MTV videos at the end of the day. A prime concern of any journalism class or unit is to help students become intelligent consumers of these messages. As students learn news values—what makes news news—they better understand why some stories merit large headlines on page one and others are treated as briefs, or why television gives big play to a visual event but a newspaper may not. They see how significance, timeliness, and human interest play roles in determining what information they receive. They evaluate news sources and decide who is credible and who is not, what information contains support and what does not. When students shift from viewing news alone to viewing news in company with various persuasive genres—advertising, editorials, reviews—they learn to spot opinion and bias, e.g., the psychological appeals ad agencies use to make readers think this product will make people popular and that one will make them safer. All are messages that students will be deciphering throughout their lives, and clues about how to do this help students become better critical thinkers.

A Dozen Media Comparison Activities for Comprehending, Interpreting, Evaluating, and Appreciating Texts

By Candace Perkins Bowen and Susan Hathaway Tantillo

- Compare, contrast, and analyze front pages from competing newspapers in the same metropolitan area for story selection, story display, story angle, and sources used. Cities with more than one daily newspaper include Chicago, Washington, D.C., Boston, Detroit, and New York.
- Compare, contrast, and analyze Web sites from competing newspapers in the same metropolitan area for story selection, story

Standard 3

display, story angle, and sources used. A list of newspaper Web sites is available from the Poynter Institute for Media Studies at http://www.poynter.org/research/jsites/je_direct.htm.

- Compare and contrast your local daily or weekly newspaper front page with the nearest metropolitan daily newspaper and analyze story selection, story display, story angle, and sources used.

- Compare and contrast the Web site for your local daily or weekly newspaper with the Web site for the nearest metropolitan daily newspaper and analyze story selection, story display, story angle, and sources used.

- Compare, contrast, and analyze reviews of the same movie, book, play, musical, compact disc, or TV show from at least two different publications. Consider reviewer opinion, writing style, and credibility.

- Compare, contrast, and analyze national and local prime-time TV newscasts for the same day for selection, time devoted to each story, order in which stories are presented, story angle, and sources used. How does CNN fit in? What about the role of Web sites in daily news coverage, such as those for MSNBC (http://www.msnbc.com), the *Christian Science Monitor* (http://csmonitor.com/), and CNN (http://www.cnn.com/)?

- Compare, contrast, and analyze a news story and a staff editorial on the same topic from the same publication.

- Compare, contrast, and analyze teen magazine coverage of the same topics covered in a magazine intended for general circulation, e.g., *Teen People* versus *People*, or *Sports Illustrated for Kids* versus *Sports Illustrated*.

- Ask fellow students to assign a letter grade to current movies and compare their ratings to those published in grid form in *Entertainment Weekly*, either in the printed magazine or on the Web site at http://www.ew.com/. [At the Web site, students can access the ratings by gender, region of the country, education, and age group, as well as cast their own votes.]

- Read a *Consumer Reports* treatment of a product that holds interest for teenagers, such as portable music players. Compare, contrast, and analyze the presentation of the testing results with the content of a single product review, such as one about an iPod, in a newspaper or magazine. [Students can get ideas at the *Consumer Reports* Web site at http://www.consumerreports.org/, but they may need to find the printed version of the report in order to read it in its entirety.]

- Compare, contrast, and analyze a variety of print advertisements or TV commercials to determine the types of persuasion techniques they use, such as the bandwagon approach, glittering generalities, testimonials, flag waving, and straightforward presentation of information.

- Read a *Consumer Reports* analysis of a product that holds interest for teenagers and is promoted through print advertisements and TV infomercials (such as an abdominal exerciser). Compare, contrast, and analyze the presentation of the *Consumer Reports* testing results with the advertising approaches. [Students can get ideas at the *Consumer Reports* Web site at http://www.consumerreports.org/, but they may need to find the printed version of the report in order to read it in its entirety.]

Organizing a Story

By Susan Hathaway Tantillo

Once students have gathered information for a story that will be longer than a news brief, the teacher/adviser can plan a lesson to introduce the different types of organization that students will encounter in professional newspapers or newsmagazines.

Four Basic Types of Organization

- Inverted pyramid—story begins with a summary or direct lead and then develops the details from most important to least important; a reader could stop almost anywhere in the story and still know the most important facts.
- Storytelling pattern—story is told in narrative form, with a beginning, middle, and end, and uses dialogue, vivid description (often involving the senses), development of character, and plot much like a piece of fiction does. It may begin with a specific scene and return to that scene at the end. A reader cannot stop reading without missing important facts.
- Chronological order—story uses time as its obvious organizational pattern: a year-by-year, month-by-month, day-by-day, hour-by-hour, minute-by-minute, or second-by-second account of an event. Within this format, it often uses characteristics of the storytelling pattern, and, as with that pattern, a reader cannot stop reading without missing important facts.
- Combination of the above.

Ideally, the teacher or adviser finds a model of each type (from professional media or student exchange papers or yearbooks from other schools), divides the beginning journalism class or publication staff into groups, and gives one story to each group. All members of each group must read the assigned story and decide which basic type it represents. Next, each group draws a visual representation of the story's organization on an overhead transparency and prepares to explain this to the class. At the end of the lesson, all students receive copies of each story, with the source noted at the top, to use as a model for the future. Once all students have had a chance to read all the stories, students can consider the following questions—first in their groups and then in an all-class discussion.

1. Which type of story do you think is the easiest to write? Hardest? Why?
2. For what topics do you think this type of story would be best? Worst? Why?
3. Which story interested you the most? Least? Was this because of the topic or because of the organization?
4. Which type of organization will you use to guide your writing of your next assignment? Why?

If time allows, the teacher could assign a follow-up activity for each student to find and bring to class another story and be prepared to explain its organization and how effective or ineffective it is.

Standard 4

Students adjust their use of spoken, written, and visual language (e.g., conventions, style, vocabulary) to communicate effectively with a variety of audiences and for different purposes.

Using Journalism

This is the very heart of journalistic writing. Students must write everything from news briefs about the French Club's trip overseas to an in-depth analysis of the school board's new Code of Conduct. They must know the difference between writing these for the PTA newsletter, which wants to promote them, the school newspaper, which wants to present them as timely news and analysis, and the yearbook, which will serve as a factual history. Journalism students must also learn to write strong editorials that present their reasons for, say, not supporting adoption of that version of the Code, along with suggestions for how to improve it. In addition, they need to write entertaining features for first-year students and other stories that appeal to seniors preparing for college. In all these articles, they must follow correct spelling, grammar, and style since they are not only the writers but the editors as well. No one will correct a spelling error between the time a story goes on the page for the commercial printer and when it comes out in homeroom the next week. And a reporter with a byline doesn't want to look foolish.

Illustrating Passive Voice with Actions

By H. L. Hall

Who said learning grammar can't be fun? The dynamic, hands-on atmosphere in a journalism class provides the right setting to cover even complicated concepts such as passive and active voice, yet do so in an entertaining way. In addition, students can then apply what they have learned to communicate more effectively with their print and broadcast audiences. While passive voice is wordier and thus newspaper editors frown on its use, those who write television and radio news copy object to it even more. A listener needs to know the "who" of the action before he or she can appreciate the "what." Professional broadcast journalists learn that S-V-O (subject-verb-object) is almost always the rule.

Students need reinforcement to grasp this concept. Involving students in a "show-and-tell" type of learning experience enables them to quickly discern the differences. After the teacher has given various examples of active- and passive-voice sentences to the class, he or she then performs some type of action for or to one of the students. Then, using first an active-voice sentence and then a passive-voice one, he or she describes what just occurred. For example, the teacher might compliment the student for doing well on a previous written assignment: "Ashley, you really wrote the news story on college night extremely well" (active voice). Then: "Ashley, that news story you turned in yesterday was written extremely well" (passive). The teacher and students then analyze the two versions.

Next, each student in the room takes a turn doing something for or to another student and telling what happened in an active sentence and then in a passive one. For example, Tyler might sharpen Joy's pencil. Tyler would then say, "I sharpened Joy's pencil" (active). And he might continue, "Joy's pencil was sharpened by me" (passive). Each student in the room completes an action and uses active and passive voice to describe it.

Three guidelines exist. First, students may not do anything harmful to one another. Second, they may not repeat any action someone else has done. This forces them to stretch their minds and become more creative as they participate in this visual and oral activity. For example, if a student gives another student a book, no other student may "give" a student something. They need to think of better action verbs as the activity continues. And third, each student must get out of his or her seat and go to the other student who is part of the action, adding to the liveliness and creativity of the class.

For follow-up, the teacher might want to assign ten active-voice sentences and their parallel passive-voice versions, with each being at least ten words long. Because this is journalism class, the teacher might require correct Associated Press style. For example:

> (Active) Senior Bob Matthews embarrassed himself when he tripped over a book bag on his way to math class, Dec. 10.
>
> (Passive) A book bag was tripped over by Bob Matthews, senior, on his way to math class, Dec. 10.

When students turn in the assignment the next day, the teacher might use peer editing in groups of three or four. Each of the students in the group looks at his or her classmates' papers and indicates whether the sentences are really active and passive as labeled. Then each group can decide which sentences convey information best. Students will quickly see, with the awkward passive sentences, why journalists prefer active voice.

Using Research to Create a "Newspaper"

By Candace Perkins Bowen

When the sophomore English class finished reading *Julius Caesar*, it was time to learn a little more about Shakespeare's life and the world he lived in. The teacher knew that traditional research often yielded stiff and boring reports from her classes. She even had to spend time researching on her own, just to assure herself that students didn't "borrow" the information too liberally without attributing it. Also, she needed to fit into an already tight schedule some practice in other forms of nonfiction writing. Her solution: The Elizabethan Newspaper.

In this unit, students form groups of four or five and take roles as the staff of a London daily in the time of Queen Elizabeth. Within that framework, they choose the publication's name and date. Content must include the range of journalistic story types all newspapers have. Other authentic bonuses can include advertising—both display and classified—as well as mock photos and other illustrations, columns, reviews, and anything else typical of today's newspapers. In other words, students do not have to study the content of newspapers in the seventeenth century, nor do they have to use the unfamiliar language conventions of four hundred years ago. They simply gather the appropriate information and write it as today's journalists would.

The assignment sheet they receive reads as follows:

> Assume you and your colleagues form the staff of the *London Daily* or another paper in that city in the early 1600s—you can choose the exact date based on the stories you wish to cover. You're producing the Sunday paper, so you must work together to create a balanced publication—some news, sports, features, whatever a newspaper has.
>
> Each reporter must write at least one story and should contribute to the publication in other ways, too. To complete your article(s), you must research a topic so it is historically "correct"— that is, even if you don't know such an event happened to this specific person, it is historically accurate in that events like it did occur at that time and in that place. Each student will hand in his or her own article(s) with a bibliography of at least three sources attached; articles will be graded on use of research information, correct journalistic style, creativity, and mechanics.
>
> Then each group will compile all articles and any art, ads, or the like, and turn in its finished "publication." It's fun to make it look like a real newspaper, either through desktop publishing or cut-and-paste, but this is not a requirement. Publications will be graded on balance and range of topics, depth of research, writing style, and creativity.

Standard 4 29

Three activities occur almost simultaneously when the project begins. First, student staffs meet and begin deciding what kind of stories they want to write. Then, or to some degree concurrently, they research and gather the facts they need for these stories. And, during class periods, they receive instruction in the basics of writing news, features, and editorials. These instructions need not be complicated. For instance, students learn:

News Story

- Purpose is to inform.
- Begins with a summary lead—the 5 Ws & H (who, what, when, where, why, and how).
- Uses inverted pyramid form, going from most important to least important.
- Has *no* reporter opinion.
- Attributes all facts to sources, e.g.:

    "Elizabeth died very peacefully," Lady Catherine Cross, her attendant, said.

    "Her illness was caused by . . . ," Dr. Geoffrey Smythe, her physician, said.

- Uses short paragraphs—generally, twenty-five to thirty words and one or two sentences.

Feature Story

- Purpose is to entertain.
- Begins with an attention-catching lead using one of the following approaches:

    | anecdote | description | direct quote |
    | surprising statement | definition | question |

- Then has a "nut graph"—the heart of the story—to sum up the focus.
- May use a more informal, relaxed style than a news story, depending on the topic.
- Uses plenty of quotes to catch the flavor of a person being profiled or the topic covered.
- Includes many types, e.g., personality profile, fashion, trend, how-to, news-based angle.
- Still has no reporter opinion.

Editorials and Commentaries

- Editorials express the opinion of the staff or editorial board, use "we," and have no byline (writer's name).

- Commentaries express one person's opinion and *do* have a by-line. In fact, they often even have a mug shot (head-and-shoulders photograph) of the writer.
- Both types are designed to persuade.
- Both provide facts, figures, experts' quotes, and so on to support their viewpoints.
- Both include the other side(s) of a controversy—and then show why it is (or they are) not valid.
- Both may begin with a lead that grabs the reader's attention, but they soon make it clear what the writer's/staff's stand is.

Certain topics are easy to cover. Some students write news stories about Elizabeth's death, placing the date of their publication in 1603. Before students begin to write, they must learn how she died and all the historical details relating to this, which they find with standard research methods. But their need to turn this into a news story—with a short summary lead, inverted pyramid form, and "expert sources" to quote—ensures that the language and organization cannot resemble what they read in history books or encyclopedias. Most articles about this news item address when and how Elizabeth died and include some quotes from the (fictional) doctor and ladies in waiting who attended her. A news story might begin:

> The reign of Queen Elizabeth has come to an end. On March 24, she passed away at 1:30 a.m.
> The Royal Physician, Dr. Alex Smith, reports her death was the result of a severe cold. "Her Highness, may her soul rest in peace, had been battling a flu. This sickness took its toll on her aged but otherwise remarkably healthy body."

Other news stories work as well, as long as depicted events are historically accurate—or at least possible at that time:

> Cobbler Jacob Edwards was taken into custody this morning by county authorities for allegedly killing two deer and a red-tailed fox in the royal forest north of town.
> "Killing of any animal within the limits of any land set aside for royal use is strictly prohibited and is certainly punishable by death," Sheriff William Paxton said.

Some stories, such as that one, can be long and detailed, with, in this case, quotes from Edwards, explanation of what the punishment might be, and even a plea from the family for donations to "help them make ends meet until Edwards goes to trial." Other stories are briefs, such as news about an arrest for "the theft of three loaves of bread" and injuries from a runaway horse and buggy.

Feature stories range from recipes for "Lovefeast Buns," "Strumbendles," and fig conserve to details on building a castle. Fashion articles are a natural:

> European designs are pouring in from Italy, France, Spain and other areas, creating what could be called the period of extremes in costume design. Now London designers are refining those looks to make them truly English.
>
> According to fashion designer Robert Sydney, who recently held his 15th annual fashion show in London, "A complete outfit consists of a chemise-smock, then a petticoat of very rich material. Next a laced bodice with 'busks,' which are often carved, and a skirt, which is padded and stiffened around the hips in a bumrawle is what every fashionable London lady needs."

Sports coverage, too, is a possibility, though students find that harder to research. Bear baiting, however, was popular in that era and works as a sports feature. These stories require gathering details and facts and using them in an inventive way with the new (i.e., journalistic) writing style students have just learned.

> The crowds were lively Friday night as two new bears were introduced at Bear Garden.
>
> The black bears, brought from Denmark by English sailors, were sold to the Canterbury Entertainment Theatre for six pounds each.
>
> During the fights, the bears were allowed to fight each other and a wild bull before being blinded and tied to a post in the middle of the theatre area.
>
> Tickets for next week's Bear Garden shows can be bought at the Canterbury or Thornhill Theatre shops.

Editorials could plead for tighter security in a London full of crime, decry debtors' prisons, or praise Elizabeth for all she accomplished. Other opinion pieces might include reviews of the latest Shakespearean play or something by one of the Bard's rivals—both, of course, requiring that the student read the play.

Even rather unusual research can come out of this assignment, some of it requiring a great deal of searching, but with more the feel of a treasure hunt than of academic research: What are typical English names? What are some towns and villages near London? How much would a horse cost in 1603?

Common Criminals Becoming Uncommonly Common

By Kirin Kalia, St. Charles (Illinois) High School

They are everywhere: in dark alleys, on the highway, in the country villages. They are minstrels, soldiers, scholars, and actors. They are the moldy spots in the fruit of English society. They are scattered all over the world, but why are there so many vagabonds in the Queen's Kingdom?

According to Timothy Leary, warden of the public jail in Boroughport, "Greater plenty breeds more envy and greed among those who feel excluded."

But this is only one of many factors contributing to the crime problem. "We released many unsavory characters when the monastery closed. I am too afraid to know what some of those men are doing now," stated James Clifton, former caretaker of the monastery in Devonshire.

The old monastery in Devonshire has not been the only one to close its doors. In recent years, monasteries throughout England have had to take this course of action, consequently leaving many formerly "harmless parasites" to roam the country.

In addition to the shrinking number of monasteries, farmers are also selling their land. They and their hired help have had to abandon rural areas in order to find work in the cities. Many of these people are poor and are willing to do anything for money. "What else can I do to survive?" said one man who calls himself George. George has only been in London for a few weeks and has already picked his share of pockets.

Another source of criminals comes from groups of wandering soldiers. These men have drifted home after fighting in France and Flanders. "They were probably vagrants or real jailbirds when they enlisted," said Leary.

Austin Fredricks, a constable, has another explanation. "After the roistering life of the camps, they have gained an even greater distaste for honest work. They are strong of arm and despise us [constables], and can make horrid disturbance of peaceful life—especially in the inland villages," he said.

Although an estimated 12,000 begging poor live in London (almost one tenth of the population), many are not criminals. Throughout the kingdom there are at least 10,000 outlaws. About 300 to 400 "are eaten up by the gallows every year," according to Leary. ▶

Matthew Longhorn, an attorney in London, thinks that if all these criminals could be organized into an army, "They could give the Queen's most powerful enemy a strong battle."

However, Longhorn noted that this type of arrangement is highly unlikely. "So many rogues go scathless all the year long that it is a mere turn of fortune if one of them is entrapped," he said.

But what is Parliament doing to punish these vagrants? According to Clarence Bigby, a member of Parliament, "We are currently doing everything we possibly can. We have already passed strict laws concerning the heinous conduct of English rogues."

Yet Clara Whitley stressed the fact that the actions of Parliament are not good enough. "Nothing happened to the villain who invaded my yard and stole my fine linens. My husband was robbed on the highway by a wandering minstrel betwixt Dover and Berwick. No one has captured the perpetrator. Where is justice? There is a vast difference between passing an Act of Parliament and seeing it enforced by the constables," she declared.

The vagabonds Whitley described are only a few of the types roaming the kingdom. Some rogues get money from soft-hearted people by pretending to have epilepsy or by displaying artificial sores. Others have forged begging licenses and say they are crippled in order to receive charity.

"Nick" earns his living by pretending to be an actor. "It's quite simple, actually," he said. "All I need is a barn, an interesting costume, and a sales pitch. For instance, 'twas last week when I announced I was putting on a tragedy. Fairly soon, all the villagers found out and arrived promptly at dusk. The only tragedy performed that night was me running away with their money. I always have the last laugh," he chuckled.

Another practicing rascal is "Spencer." He prefers to beg for school fees outside Oxford University with his forged license. "Sure there are chaps who sincerely need money. But I am as needy as any of them. They need money for school. I need it for a living. Who dares to say that they are more clever than I? I can outsmart any of those imbeciles, especially when it comes to the law," he asserted.

This adventurous spirit still burns furiously amongst the dirtiest English scoundrels.

Longhorn commented, "As he [a rogue] sits in the stocks or even as he mounts the gallows, he will probably curse his ill luck rather than reflect that honesty is the best policy."

Vignette: Adapting to a Varied Audience

By Michele Dunaway

In many cases, middle school journalists have used only written language to communicate with their teachers in other courses, but they must eventually learn to become experts at adjusting their use of spoken, written, and visual language to communicate effectively with a variety of audiences and for different purposes.

Students at Rockwood South Middle School learned this truth in several very concrete ways. At the beginning of the school year, the newspaper staff conducted a survey about smoking. The survey revealed that while 70 to 80 percent of seventh and eighth graders who responded had tried smoking, only 20 percent of the sixth graders had done so. A follow-up survey on alcohol yielded similar numbers.

Therefore, students knew they had two different audiences who would read their newspaper articles. There were the younger, "more innocent" sixth graders and the older, "more experienced" eighth graders. When writing any story, the eighth-grade students on the newspaper staff had to work beyond just making sure their writing was clear and concise. They needed to make certain that the language they used and, specifically, the words they chose reached both audiences. For this reason, they turned down a drug awareness story that sounded more like a manual: "If you get high, the symptoms you'll experience are...." The staff was also careful about the way it covered a suicide and another student death. Aware of the risk of copycat suicides, no mention of cause went in the first obituary. When the second death occurred, it was reported in a similar fashion. Covering school safety in the wake of the Columbine shootings also required a sensitivity to readers' ages and attitudes. (See sidebar story below.)

Students also carefully chose and adjusted their language when writing editorials. Some editorials praise, while others criticize and offer constructive solutions. Editorials had to be written so they didn't sound like whining—a typical reaction for eighth-grade students is to draw up a petition on a scrap sheet of paper—yet the editorial needs to clearly assert its point and let the reader feel the newspaper has spoken for or against an issue.

Lastly, every time students went on interviews, they modified the way they spoke. Interviewing administrators called for a more formal approach and language, while interviewing students called for the interviewer to use a more casual, peer-to-peer style.

School Safety Concerns All Students

By Megan Henderson, Rockwood South Middle School, Fenton, Missouri

While shots were ringing through the halls at Columbine High School, several members of the newspaper staff and I were crammed into a van, making the three-hour trip back to St. Louis from an all-day Missouri Interscholastic Press Association journalism conference in Columbia.

We were all excited because our school newspaper had just been named All-Missouri. As we listened to sketchy details of the tragedy on the radio, we came down to earth and knew that we had a story on our hands that we had to cover.

School safety is an issue that concerns all students, and earlier in the school year we had covered the suspension of students who had brought a BB gun on the bus. The editors and staff felt our readers needed to be aware of what was being done at our school to avoid an incident like Columbine's happening at our school, which is located in a suburb of St. Louis.

Our staff worked hard to produce a paper that focused on many aspects of the shooting. We included an editorial urging students to report any threats of violence to an administrator and a positive book review of *Chicken Soup for the Teenage Soul*, and we evaluated the effect the media have on violent teenagers. We even localized the school shootings issue with an article describing the suspension of a Rockwood South student who made threatening statements referring to the Littleton incident, and we covered Rockwood South's first campus intruder drill.

Knowing that school safety is a controversial, serious issue, we took precautions to make sure the issue offended no one. Although we are not held to the system of prior review, we still decided to have Principal Gary Drummond evaluate the pages before we went to press.

The staff understood that the *RAMpage* reaches students as young as sixth graders, and we wanted to make sure we were not actually inciting violence in our attempt to prevent it. When Drummond didn't find any problems with the material, we sent the paper off to be printed.

Our feeling of pride as we distributed the 14-page issue quickly turned into dread as critical reviews came pouring in. Staff members would return from delivering a stack of papers to report that several teachers seemed less than enthusiastic to distribute the paper to their students. One teacher sent it back and refused to distribute it at all, largely because of the depiction of a handgun on the cover.

This year our paper was trying to go for a magazine approach with a dominant piece of art and little type on the cover. The cover of our June issue had a computer reproduction of a gun and the quote, "Parting is all we know of heaven. And all we need of hell," from Emily Dickinson.

We were shocked at the negative reaction, primarily to the art, because our staff and adviser never envisioned a problem with the cover or the written material involved.

The complaint many teachers and staff members made was that the pistol on the front of the issue sent the image to students that the paper promotes gun use. However, we selected the image to make the students want to open the paper and read the articles.

We wanted to grab the readers' attentions, so they would actually read the stories that advocated safe schools and nonviolent actions. If we had thought of it, we could have put an "x" over the gun or a circle around the graphic with a line through it. The idea didn't cross our minds, though, and it seemed that the headline and quote gave out the nonviolent message we hoped to achieve.

Our goal for producing this paper was to enlighten the students of Rockwood South on the causes and effects of school violence and what they can do to prevent an episode like the Columbine shooting from happening.

It was never an option for the *RAMpage* staff to avoid coverage of the school shooting in Littleton, Colorado. We covered this controversial topic in an appropriate, tasteful manner for the age group and maturity level of our readers. While we could have done some things differently, the angle from which we presented this information may help to prevent violence—and that was our goal.

[Reprinted with permission from Communication: Journalism Education Today, *magazine of the Journalism Education Association, Winter 1999.]*

Standard 5

Students employ a wide range of strategies as they write and use different writing process elements appropriately to communicate with different audiences for a variety of purposes.

Using Journalism

The writing process is a natural part of journalism. No one states that more clearly than author, poet, journalist, and writing coach Donald Murray in his *Writing for Your Readers* (1992): "The writing process places priority on what works: Why is this story good, and what stages did the writer pass through to make the final draft effective? Good writing is magic; but if you want to know magic, you have to talk to magicians. They repeat magic, producing the impossible on schedule, and so do our best writers. Researchers of the writing process observe and question the best writers on their best stories to discover what went right" (2). Just as Murray discovered this magic through his work as a coach and as a columnist for the *Boston Globe*, students discover it through careful study of the writing process in the classroom and in their work on school newspapers.

Comparing an Editorial and a News Story

By Susan Hathaway Tantillo

"I just don't know what she wants me to do," Jamie whined after the news editor returned her news story on two teen deaths from heroin overdoses. "She just doesn't understand my story."

"Let's look at it together," Stephanie, the editor in chief, said. "What has she written on it?"

"Mostly she says I can't say any of these things about what a tragedy these deaths are and how I feel about kids who use drugs unless I quote someone else," Jamie said. "But I just don't know how to write this without putting in what I think. I was really excited about doing this front-page story about these kids who died and talking about what I know about drugs in the suburbs, but now I'm not. Julie has ruined it for me."

"Jamie, I think you should have really volunteered to write a column about these deaths and the increased use of heroin among suburban teens, instead of the front-page news story," Stephanie told her. "But now Julie is counting on you to whip this into shape for page one. Let me help. We just need to find some experts to say the same things you are saying and some other students to quote about their opinions about all this. Let's make a list of people we can talk to. Then I'll help you do the interviews tomorrow. Okay?"

Jamie agreed reluctantly: "I guess so, but it's still not the same story I wanted to write."

Apparently Jamie had missed the journalism class lesson on the difference between a straight news story or a news feature and an opinion piece related to a timely topic. She and Stephanie managed to interview and include quotes from two students, the school psychologist, and the school's police liaison officer, who formerly worked with the Drug Abuse Resistance Education (DARE) program. They also quoted a section from the school's student handbook regarding drug use.

To produce a student newspaper that accomplishes all the purposes of the media—to inform, to influence, to entertain, and to serve—the student staff and their adviser must be sure to include all types of stories. Except on pages where readers expect content to express the writer's opinion, such as editorials, columns or letters on the editorial page, and reviews in the entertainment section, stories must be presented by the writers as objectively as humanly possible. To do that, student journalists need to see themselves as messengers who deliver ideas they have gathered from others. They should not interject their own ideas or their own biases into their stories.

The best way to accomplish this objectivity is to be good *reporters*. As the word "reporter" indicates, the writer must gather information from sources and then communicate that information—make a report—to the readers. To be as objective as possible, reporters make lists of sources to contact to represent all possible points of view or sides of a given story. They then interview these persons, making sure to fairly represent all viewpoints. Reporters may do this through a combination of direct quotes and indirect quotes, but they must cite the names and identifications of the sources they use so their readers can know who said what.

And, because we are talking about student publications here, student journalists should interview fellow students who are willing to voice their opinions on the various sides of the story at hand. Student journalists who do not seek out the views of fellow students to include in their stories are missing one of their unique student journalist opportunities—giving fellow students a voice.

Personal journalism, including opinion writing, certainly has a place in the scholastic press, but students need to realize when they are writing opinion and confine those pieces to the opinion pages or to clearly labeled pieces in other sections of the newspaper. In short, they must learn how to write for different purposes. And school publications are a terrific microcosm in which to do this.

Vignette: Reporting on the Witch's Trial

By Candace Perkins Bowen

Leeanne Alsept received a teaching bonus when her sister Jill Martin and Jill's classmate Joe Paris volunteered to teach a journalism unit in her class as a project for their university methods course. Her gifted fifth graders at Claymont Middle School in Dennison, Ohio, had been using *Fairy Tales on Trial* by Janis Silverman. After studying a group of well-known tales, the students decided that "Hansel and Gretel" best illustrated criminal behavior—from the children, who trespassed and lied, to the obvious villain, the witch. With background from a local attorney who talked to the students, they followed proper procedures to arrest and charge her and put her on trial. To help students get ready for that phase, the attorney also helped some students prepare her defense, presenting her as a "sort of Good Witch Glenda like [in] *The Wizard of Oz*," Alsept said. Yes, they said, she is a witch, but she isn't guilty of this evil deed.

Jill and Joe then presented the basics of newswriting: The lead needs to have the five Ws and H—who, what, when, where, why, and how. After that summary beginning, the story needs to be written in an inverted pyramid with the most important information at the top and the least important at the bottom. "This," as Jill explained to the class, "allows the editor to cut the story if it doesn't fit in the space that's available." They also told the fifth graders that news stories need quotes to help support the facts, and they showed examples.

To gather the information they needed in order to write a news story, students conducted a press conference with the witch. Alsept thinks that viewing several press conferences before they staged one on their own would help in the future, but students got the right idea even so, Paris said. Finally, they paired up to write the stories. Two of the groups used computers available in the classroom and tried to make theirs look like newspaper stories.

Most groups wrote with little additional instruction, while others needed more guidance. For instance, Paris said one pair had a hard time getting started, so he prompted them by asking what to put in the lead while he wrote down what they said. Then they took off on their own.

Another group, which included the prosecuting attorney, took a unique angle and quoted her as a news source. This led to a discussion of how each group could start with the same material, yet end up with something completely different. "They definitely were conscious of audience awareness, and they learned that even though they all worked with the same information, the stories varied greatly," Paris said.

Mrs. Broomstick's Brewing Dilemma

By Heath Manbeck and Stephen Tripp, Claymont Middle School, Dennison, Ohio

At a press conference this morning at 8:45 A.M. in Dennison, Ohio, Mrs. Broomstick was questioned regarding her upcoming trial, which accused her of kidnapping and attempting murder of Hansel and Gretel.

Mrs. Broomstick, a former inhabitant of a deserted island in the middle of nowhere, now lives in the enchanted forest in Illinois.

When asked about the accusations she replied, "I like children and would never eat them because I only eat chicken." She claims her and her sister are both "good" witches.

She was shocked when Gretel pushed her in the oven because she claims she only was taking good care of them and feeding them because they were hungry.

When asked about her unusual house made from cake, she said, "I baked a really big cake for it to be eaten by the forest animals and little children."

She plans to build a new house after the trial so "kids wouldn't try to prosecute (her)."

> **Accused Witch Clears Her Name**
>
> **By Lauren Welch and Leah Addison, Claymont Middle School, Dennison, Ohio**
>
> At 8:45 this morning, Ms. Broomstick held a press conference in Dennison, Ohio, to clear her name of the charges of Conspiracy and attempted Murder, child Abduction, Kidnapping, Confinement against one's will, Forcible Detention, and Unlawful Restraint.
>
> "She is doing real well with answering questions," said Attorney Leah Addison. "I think she may have a chance on winning that trial on Tuesday."
>
> Still, charges are strong.

Works Cited

Murray, Donald. 1992. *Writing for Your Readers: Notes on the Writer's Craft from the* Boston Globe. 2nd edition. Old Saybrook, Conn.: Globe Pequot.

Silverman, Janis L. 1999. *Fairy Tales on Trial.* Dayton, Ohio: Pieces of Learning.

Standard 6

Students apply knowledge of language structure, language conventions (e.g., spelling and punctuation), media techniques, figurative language, and genre to create, critique, and discuss print and nonprint texts.

Using Journalism

Journalists are concerned with the whole package they prepare for readers and viewers. For instance, through publishing, they learn that language conventions do matter. When their school newspaper stories have spelling and grammar errors, readers notice and comment. When they organize a magazine article without giving necessary background, readers are confused and don't continue to the end. When they use sarcasm to make a point, they learn that the audience response is different than it is when they use direct argumentation. In addition, they learn what *does* work when an editorial campaign brings about a positive change in their school, when community leaders ask student journalists to join them on an important task force, or even when the halls are abuzz with comments about a good investigative article.

Vignette: Collaborating on an Editorial

By Lisa O. Greeves

For one unit on editorials in a Journalism 1 survey class, students study and discuss sample editorials from both professional and student newspapers and then select an editorial topic for the class as a whole to write on. For instance, in one recent class, which took place at a time when tightened security and various associated changes were a current issue of hot debate, students selected "school security" as the editorial topic. The assistant principal and school security director received invitations to come separately to the class for group question-and-answer sessions on the topic. Then, two classes ahead of time, the students and adviser brainstormed potential ideas and questions for students to address during these sessions. All students were expected to take notes and ask questions in a professional, controlled fashion.

After the class members engaged in their initial brainstorming of ideas and issues to cover in this editorial, they assigned several students to research statistics and facts in a wide variety of related areas. Students produced information on children carrying and using guns, numbers of people who die violently each year in American schools, numbers of students expelled for bringing guns to their public schools, and some commentary on exaggerations made about children carrying weapons.

Another group of students researched the school's copy of the Fairfax County Public Schools' School Board Regulations for specific language and guidelines regarding school security rules to help them determine where the school might be violating county code. On a related point, the assistant principal revealed during the students' group interview with him that the individual school can modify the security regulations within reason.

Then students sought additional material in another way. School administrators had recently begun locking doors during the day, so students requested time during class to monitor outside doors for a thirty-minute period to count the number of violations.

Prepared with all of this information, the group devoted a class period to agreeing on an organization for the editorial, as well as choosing the overall stand. At that point, they broke into groups, with each composing one part of the editorial and, in sequence, entering it into the computer, which is attached to a twenty-six-inch television screen in the classroom so the words appear on the screen as they are keyboarded. The rest of the students could critique and comment as the process progressed.

The editorial changed greatly as the class worked on it together, yielding some intense discussions about language, strategy, and rhetoric. Stopping many times to read aloud what they had created together, the students could hear the effect of what they had composed to help them critique better. The atmosphere was quite casual, with some groups typing, others writing together, and still others reading and commenting about what appeared onscreen. Students saw clearly that a one-shot draft would have limited effectiveness, and they wrote three drafts before they were satisfied.

Gradually, as the editorial began to take shape and the students modified their writing and the overall structure of the piece, they decided after great discussion that the research on national violence statistics did not fit with the direction their editorial was taking. They chose to keep the piece focused on the individual situation of their school as opposed to blending in national information; they also felt that including those national statistics might turn the editorial into a "scare" piece, which they wanted to avoid. And they felt that the use of those statistics would be a little too typical, would be too similar to other editorials written in the same vein. But they realized that gathering this kind of research was part of ensuring that they, as writers, had a good grasp of the entire situation, which could only help them during the writing and composing process. (See the related sidebar later in this chapter for the text of the first draft.)

At the end of each class, I printed out copies of what we'd written that day and distributed a copy to each student to take home to read and edit for the next class period. I checked students' papers at the beginning of class, to ensure that they'd marked them up genuinely and thoughtfully, and gave each credit for doing so. This ensured that students were getting some credit for the amount of work they were doing in class on this lengthy project and also that all students came to class having read the draft currently up for discussion at least once and that all had some thoughts on what should be done to it at that point. This ensured a high-quality discussion each day.

Changes from the First Draft to the Second Draft

Much of what we changed and added resulted from having one person read the draft aloud to the class slowly and clearly, with everyone else reading along silently on the big television screen. For each of the three drafts, we'd stop and read aloud what we'd written at least four or five times. While sometimes the students would grumble, they learned the importance of hearing what they'd written and realized that the ear can often detect problems where the eye simply skims over them, a practice I encourage in all my student writers. We drafted the editorial in a large font to ensure that everyone could easily read the words on the screen. The combination of reading and listening to how the words flowed enabled students to make decisions about what worked well and what didn't. Often they couldn't wait until the reader had read the entire editorial; they would start chiming in immediately. I encouraged them to scribble down their thoughts and to save them until we'd read the entire piece.

After hearing the draft read aloud, we cleared up some language in the first paragraph. Students changed "this school's lax attitude concerning security was a leading factor in the recent incident . . ." to "this school's lax attitude regarding security resulted in . . ." for the reason that the latter was a stronger and more direct assertion rather than beating around the bush.

Additionally, numerous debates popped up about words like "concerning" versus "regarding," with the students debating among themselves which was clearer or more to the point. We debated the use of the word "lax" and whether it was too insulting. As the teacher, I joined in these debates whenever necessary to help students decide—or encouraged them to leave the offending word for now if they couldn't come up with a solution, in order to continue making progress on the entire piece. I reminded them at times like these of the importance of not losing their momentum in writing by agonizing endlessly over one word, of the importance of revisiting that section in a later draft.

Another change between the first and the second drafts occurs in the paragraph detailing the students' "experiment" of counting people entering the front door. In the first draft, the students simply stated the process, presented the number of people counted, and quickly drew a rhetorical conclusion. After hearing it read aloud, I prompted them to discuss what they wanted to accomplish by mentioning that experiment and suggested they were giving it short shrift. After being reminded that readers are normally rather lazy, and won't do much calculating on their own, students explored in conversation how to draw the conclusion more explicitly for the reader, how to lead the reader more to what they wanted the reader to realize. As a result, they decided to make their point by projecting the numbers to cover an entire day: "Although only four people in half an hour may not seem like much, that is 64 people in an eight-hour day." It strengthened the passage immensely.

A final significant change between these first two drafts was the acknowledgment of the security assistants who helped security/safety specialist Keith Dixon throughout the day. After discussion, the students realized that they were making it sound like Dixon was the lone man guarding the homestead against coyotes when really that wasn't the case. And to be fair and accurate, they needed to acknowledge the other workers in this arena. The students also ended up providing clearer details about the security precautions that the school does use.

Changes from the Second Draft to the Third Draft

The second draft actually took a couple of class periods to bang out; students added many more details and large chunks of content and did some minor editing. But after finally producing a clear, solid, second draft, the changes made between the second and the third were very much rhetorical in scope (see the second sidebar below for the text of the third draft). For instance, in paragraph one, the next-to-last sentence became "we should not assume that we are invulnerable" as opposed to the wordier and vaguer "this should not lead us to believe that we are invulnerable." Also, a finalization of the editorial's stand appears in the last sentence of the lead, which changed to "This school and its student body must reevaluate . . ." as opposed to the previous "This school must reevaluate . . . ." The students, after reading their drafts over and over and discussing them for several days, finally realized they needed to include themselves, as students, as the targeted audience of this piece instead of resorting to a vague pointing of fingers at "the school." They learned a great lesson about audience, the placing of blame and its power in an editorial, and clarifying vague language all at the same time.

Other strong rhetorical changes that emerged in draft three included a more formal way of leading into the explanation of their experiment—"The February intrusion prompted an informal survey of who enters our doors and wanders our halls"—as opposed to the sentence from the first two drafts that relied on use of the word "we." The students discussed at length using "we" and wondered how the reader of this hypothetical editorial would ever know who "we" was. Again, a meaningful discussion allowed them to teach themselves a strong writing lesson that could even cross disciplines into regular expository writing.

In addition, the order of sentences and content in the middle of the editorial was pruned and organized much better in the third draft. The students had commented several times during the reading of draft two that while they liked a particular sentence or thought, they had a feeling it simply wasn't in the right place but couldn't quite figure out where it needed to go in order to flow better. Many passages improved as a result of attention to order. For instance, in the paragraph beginning "This school strictly enforces its own safety policy . . . ," the rest of this first sentence was removed, thus allowing the paragraph to focus on the positive steps the school was taking in terms of security. The part that was omitted, ". . . but for a high tech high school, the security measures don't quite measure up," was a phrasing the students *loved* and were reluctant to part with. They commented many times during discussion about the play on words in that phrasing and how strong it sounded. However, as discussions went on and the editorial took on a more refined shape and organization, they realized this phrasing was in the wrong place, since it split up a section that focused on positives, and thus it really didn't belong. Again, they learned a good lesson about revising—that writers must often part with words they really like and that they often need to look at a piece of writing many, many times in order to see it clearly.

Finally, the students ended up revising the paragraph that starts to lead in to criticisms about the school's security, which follow the positives paragraph. They softened the tone and ensured that they created a sense of acknowledging the special circumstances that surround the special "culture" of our particular magnet school. This paragraph, which begins with "Granted, we lack the more overt and proactive precautions taken at other schools," eventually served as a solid transition to the criticism and the heart of the students' editorial stand and resulted from much detailed, minute discussion of specific words (like "Granted") and specific questioning about what we wanted to accomplish in that paragraph.

The technology involved in this lesson plan, specifically the use of the presentation station, allows basic, solid lessons in writing and revising to be illustrated on a literal level. The students see what needs to be done in a way that they often don't see in their own papers and from teachers' limited comments in the margins. The informal, comfortable setting of students gathered around a television screen, along with the use of small groups of students composing sections together, allows and encourages larger group discussions, something that is key to teaching lessons on writing. Students should be able to draw conclusions from what they discussed about the composing process during this modeling lesson and apply them to their own writing assignments on an individual basis.

When complete, the editorial went to the assistant principal and the security director, who had cooperated with the assignment and said they were happy to have been asked. Although almost two weeks of class time went into the activity, the hands-on interviewing, writing, and discussing drew positive comments from the students.

Group Editorial—First Draft

Journalism 1 / Mrs. Greeves
Thomas Jefferson High School for Science and Technology
Alexandria, Virginia

We all have heard more than once the phrase: "Oh, but it's TJ," or "just leave it on top of your locker." However, this school's lax attitude regarding security was a leading factor in the recent incident when a girl was followed into the restroom by an unidentified male. The man was able to enter and leave the school without suspicion. While this school does experience a minimal amount of security concerns, this should not lead us to believe that we are invulnerable. It's high time that this school and its student body re-evaluate its attitude concerning security.

In addition to the incident last week, this school has not been immune to problems in the past. Last year, there were well-publicized cases of locker room theft. Shortly after the Columbine shootings, a ticking briefcase was found outside the front office, although it was later determined to be a prank. A few years ago a student was suspended for several days for inadvertently spraying his friends with mace.

In the past outsiders have been able to enter this school with ease. Last year, four students from another school, acting as a gang, entered this school and damaged some vending machines. For a number of years, car parts, most notably radios, were stolen from parked cars in this school's parking lots.

Faced with these incidents of breached security, measures didn't quite measure up. During the day, the security system consists of a vigilant Security/Safety Specialist Keith Dixon patrolling the hallways for unidentified visitors. Anyone caught without proper visible identification is asked to either provide an ID badge or proceed to the office to sign in, often escorted by Dixon himself. Even if Dixon recognizes the individual as one of the 80% of the staff who do not regularly wear badges, he will still ask for verification of county employment.

Besides Dixon scouting the halls, the only other safety precautions this school has is locking doors, a security system activated at night using motion sensors, and locked gates for the access road. Except for the two main entrances and four other doors, including two leading from the health trailers, all doors are to be locked.

Group Editorial—Third Draft

Journalism 1 / Mrs. Greeves
Thomas Jefferson High School for Science and Technology
Alexandria, Virginia

More than once we have heard the phrases: "Oh, but it's TJ," or "Just leave it on top of your locker." However, this school's lax

▶

attitude regarding security resulted in the February 1 incident when an unidentified male followed a girl into a restroom. The man was able to enter and leave the school without suspicion. While this school experiences a minimal amount of security problems, we should not assume that we are invulnerable. This school and its student body must reevaluate its perspective concerning security.

In addition to the incident last month, this school has encountered security problems in the past. Last year, there were multiple cases of locker room theft. Shortly after the Columbine incident, a ticking briefcase was found outside the front office, although it was later determined to be a prank. Outsiders have also been able to enter this school with ease. Last year, four students from another school, acting as a gang, entered this school and vandalized vending machines. For a number of years, portable CD players and CDs were stolen from the inside of parked cars.

The February intrusion prompted an informal survey of who enters our doors and wanders our halls. During the thirty-minute time period, four adults without visible identification entered the school and did not follow the proper procedure of signing in at the main office. Moreover, their entrance was not hindered in any way by any member of the school community. Though four people in half an hour may seem insignificant, four people every half hour for the length of the school day adds up to 64 people in one day. All it takes is one of those individuals to cause a problem.

This school strictly enforces its own safety policy. During the day, the security system consists of vigilant Security and Safety Specialist Keith Dixon and Assistant Security and Safety Specialists Dave Sneddon and Elaine Schumacher patrolling the hallways for unidentified visitors. Besides Dixon and his assistants scouting the halls, the only other daytime safety precautions at this school are locking doors and locked gates for the access road. At night, the security system uses motion sensors.

Granted, we lack the more overt and proactive precautions taken at other schools. We are the only high school in the county that does not have a police officer in full uniform. In addition, we do not have metal detectors at our doors, locker searches, nor hall monitors. However, we do not want to compromise our culture and privileges at this school by living in a state of martial law. Therefore, our school community simply needs to be more cognizant of the circumstances that surround it.

Currently this school does not adhere to any county policies involving security. According to FCPS School Board Regulations, "all employees shall wear badges while on school property." However, Dixon estimates that only 25 of this school's 160 faculty members wear their badges. The regulations also require all visitors to "sign in and to display visitors' badges." The entranceway survey clearly revealed that this sign-in policy is not strictly followed.

The school board regulations further state that "entrance and exit shall be limited to the main entrance only." Assistant Principal John Colegrove explained how the regulations also give principals the authority to amend this policy. As a result, this school's revised security plan allows for three unlocked doors in addition to the standard main entrance.

Because of the convenience, everyone must take on more responsibility to counteract the increased potential for unwanted visitors. Teachers need to wear their badges to identify themselves. The students in turn must be more active in distinguishing visitors from faculty members and informing teachers of strangers in the building. Teachers, because they are wearing their badges, can then more easily assist individuals and direct them to the main office. Finally, students need to be as prompt as possible about informing teachers of unidentified visitors so teachers can take the appropriate actions. In the February 1 incident, the victim waited close to an hour before informing anyone of the intruder. As a result, the offender was not apprehended.

The security plan that this school has embraced sacrifices security for convenience while preserving our unique culture. Still, we cannot leave the job of maintaining this school's security to locked doors and motion sensors. Our security system can only be as effective as the students and teachers who enforce it.

Standard 7

Students conduct research on issues and interests by generating ideas and questions, and by posing problems. They gather, evaluate, and synthesize data from a variety of sources (e.g., print and nonprint texts, artifacts, people) to communicate their discoveries in ways that suit their purpose and audience.

Using Journalism

Most solid journalism uses research. Those front page news stories are not just off the top of the writer's head. In fact, it's this research that turns a writer into a journalist, a *reporter*. Today's reporters must brainstorm for topics and then select ones of interest to an audience. They don't lack for topics; the challenge is to focus on something in the barrage of information available. With a focus in mind, they use all methods at their command to gather data: from interviews to the Internet, from television to textbooks, and from observation to online publications. Then journalists are most interested in packaging their findings for their readers and viewers. Today's digital technology allows convergence in media, so the reporter can present his or her news report live through a streaming Webcast, or the videographer can capture one exciting frame and print it in the newspaper. And anyone with access to programs like PageMaker and QuarkXPress can be a publisher and present the results to an audience.

Vignette: Applying "Real-World" Research

By Donna M. Spisso

> I stepped over the gutter and ducked to pass through the doorway in the wall surrounding the cluster of ramshackle cottages which, linked together, form the Tangail brothel in Bangladesh, two hours from Dhaka. As I approached the first cottage, the women nearest the door smiled warmly at the foreigner, me, as they knelt or squatted chewing betel nut.
>
> One outstretched hand reached for my elbow to lead me over the threshold of the first cottage. The hand belonged to Lippy, who was to be my guide. She led me through narrow corridors from the first cottage to her own "home" where a makeshift bed took up half of the room and rotted dahl and biscuits in the corner kept even the flies away.

> She apologized for the poor lighting, explained that last year's cyclone had downed the power lines, forcing her to live by the natural light filtering through her tattered curtains. Even in the murky light, however, I could see the posters of Shahrukh Khan and Govinda, famous Hindi movie stars, on the wall next to a newsprint copy of a brightly colored calligraphy presenting a passage from the Holy Quran.
> Confronted with Lippy and others directly dealing with the threat and consequences of HIV/AIDS, I saw the human face attached to the disease.

Thus begins Christean's senior project on HIV/AIDS in Bangladesh. An expatriate American at the American International School/Dhaka, Christean was one of twenty-five twelfth graders in a culturally diverse class on her way to completing a seven-month research project culminating in a twenty- to thirty-page paper on an aspect of the host country which interested her. The project, which includes a twenty-minute oral presentation before an audience of peers, teachers, parents, and community members, is a graduation requirement. Accompanied by a PowerPoint presentation and other visual aids, projects have also been enhanced by student dancing, singing, artwork, photo exhibits, and newspaper articles.

Those seniors striving for an Honors distinction answer rigorous questions from a panel composed of experts in the field, a teacher, the superintendent, a school board member, and the principal. Topics have ranged from Bengali musical drama, women in journalism, the Internet, and joint families to leprosy, spousal violence, rape, and acid burn victims. No matter what the subject, all projects require original research, interviews with experts as well as those affected by the issue, and, when appropriate, site visits to hospitals, foreign aid projects, far-flung villages, and even brothels; in short, these young researchers are practicing the craft of investigative reporting.

While a social studies teacher has always taught Senior Project, the course naturally lends itself to a cross-disciplinary approach. Thus in a recent term, the senior English teacher and yearbook sponsor collaborated with the Senior Project teachers in using journalism techniques to help students put a human face on their research. After students had chosen subjects, written their purpose statements, and begun to familiarize themselves with available sources in the library and on the Internet, they learned how to conduct an interview. They started formulating "How?" and "Why?" questions, rather than the yes/no variety.

After practicing interviewing each other, students left the classroom for the "real world." They began seeking out and talking to the people who would become the richest sources for their research. Some Bangla speakers simply stepped outside the school walls to talk directly to rickshaw-wallahs about their daily routines; others visited local garment factories to interview child workers with the help of an interpreter, at all times under the watchful eye of a suspicious supervisor; still others, with good political connections, managed an audience with Khaleda Zia, Prime Minister of Bangladesh, and Raja Devasish Roy, King of the Chakma tribe in the Chittagong Hill Tracts. Students experienced the frustration of missed or postponed appointments caused by bureaucratic inefficiency, as well as the need to schedule and reschedule site visits due to nationwide transportation strikes. There was no doubt that going beyond print and electronic sources was no easy task; in fact, venturing into the real world was inconvenient, time-consuming, even intimidating at times. Nevertheless, students persevered in the pursuit of their original research. Ultimately, they were rewarded with the kind of information seldom found in history books or technical journals. Each was beginning to put a human face on his or her topic.

With several good interviews, a site visit or two, and sufficient background research under their belts, students were ready to begin writing based on their experiences in the field. First, they studied models of excellent nonfiction work by writers like George Orwell, John McPhee, and Joan Didion, as well as newspaper articles featuring skillful use of the suspended-interest lead (i.e., one that teases readers with an anecdote to draw them into the piece). They analyzed the effect of focusing on an individual as representative of an entire group of people affected by a particular problem, an increasingly common technique found in the pages of the *International Herald Tribune* and other highly respected newspapers. To begin their research papers, students imitated the models and experimented with dialogue, scenarios, narratives, and anecdotes. Like Christean, they focused on an experience in which they interacted with people directly affected by the subject they were researching. They learned that it was one thing to view a problem through statistics: "estimates of HIV-infected Bangladeshis range from 44 to 20,000 [in 1977]" but quite another to view it through the eyes of a high-risk prostitute living in a much-frequented brothel situated on a truck route on the border of Bangladesh and India. As they wrote their papers over a period of months, students learned to include charts, sidebars, graphics, and/or photos to maintain reader interest and elucidate main points. Some wove anecdotes of people they had interviewed throughout the paper, or followed a particular individual to the end. The traditional research paper, complete with footnotes and bibliography, had become more than just an academic exercise to prepare students for college.

In one instance, a student's senior project had more far-reaching effects. Fidha's report on the insidious crime of acid violence, which exists only in Bangladesh, inspired Ratna, a member of the yearbook and newspaper staffs, to interview a few of the young women whose faces had been disfigured by acid thrown on them by rejected suitors out of revenge. Her article appeared not only in the school newspaper but also prominently on page 2 of the April 1998 issue of the *International Educator,* a publication reaching thousands of teachers and administrators in the international community of independent schools. Encouraged by her journalism teacher, Ratna reworked the article to enter the contest "Profiles in Courage—Young People Who Stand Up for Their Rights," sponsored by the Newspaper Association of America Foundation. The article focused on Bina, a survivor who refused to let her tragedy keep her down, and was one of ten honorable mentions recognized at the Journalism Education Association/National Scholastic Press Association convention in Washington, D.C., in November 1998. Besides adding her voice to international coverage of acid burn violence in Bangladesh, Ratna encouraged her class to contribute its community service funds to aid the survivors. Juniors and seniors at the school continue to support the recently established Acid Burn Survivors Foundation.

Standard 8

Students use a variety of technological and informational resources (e.g., libraries, databases, computer networks, video) to gather and synthesize information and to create and communicate knowledge.

Using Journalism

Student journalists are encouraged to tap into the ever-increasing variety of sources. As they write articles, they must read background material in local newspapers, in magazines, and in specialized books. With that information, they must formulate questions and conduct interviews with local "experts," from school nurses to lawyers to the student on the street. Today's youthful reporters conduct searches on the Internet and evaluate the credibility of the information they get there, whether it's a federal database or a Web site. With all this information, student journalists write articles telling their audience what it wants and needs to know.

Gathering Internet Sources

By Richard P. Johns

With technology changing constantly, it is important for student journalists to be aware of all the sources of information available. The Internet in general, and services such as LexisNexis in particular, make a wealth of information available to students. Ten years ago, these resources were not in use like they are today. It is all the more meaningful for students to learn about such sources in order to communicate with and educate the public effectively.

Stacy, a reporter for her high school newspaper, has been assigned to track down material concerning the Clinton impeachment trial. She does a LexisNexis search and finds a great number of articles from magazines and newspapers that will help her write her story about the effect the impeachment trial has had on students in the school.

Stacy then continues to do a Web search concerning the trial. What she finds on the Web is a plethora of subjects concerning the Clinton scandal: the "Society to Impeach Clinton" Web page, the "Victims of Big Bad Bill Clinton" Web site, many others of the same type. She includes information from three or four of the Web sites in her story.

The next day, her student editor asks her, "Stacy, where'd you find this stuff?"

"Off the Web," Stacy answers.

"You had better cite where you got this stuff, or we're going to get into trouble," the editor says.

Stacy goes back to the Web but cannot find the information since she did not bookmark the pages or write down the Web site addresses.

Journalists have to be careful every day when using sources. Some sources are not as dependable as they might look; they may simply present the opinion of some radical sitting at his or her computer, making thoughts on the situation sound factual. It's tough to make the call when information found on the World Wide Web looks like it is from a "dependable" organization, such as the "Society to Impeach Clinton," when in reality it is a lone individual who creates such political sites as a hobby or crackpot endeavor. Equally unreliable are "homepages" students may use to post opinions and reports. One alert student copyeditor discovered incorrect dates in an article about Martin Luther King—and the reporter discovered he was using a seventh-grade student's history research paper to get his facts.

How do the students figure out the best way to deal with this new technology? It's not easy, which is why they must be so careful when they are using telecommunications to gather facts. Student journalists have an edge on other student researchers because their advisers and teachers have generally encouraged them to use and carefully evaluate "cyber" material since it first became available. When taking information from the Internet, like Stacy did, reporters have been taught to ask themselves, "Is this a credible source?" "Has this person cited other sources for the information presented on the site?" A site like CNN.com would be considered relatively reliable, since it is the work of a highly respected international news agency, but CNN articles have quotes as well. Reporters on the site indicate who told them what. Stacy can see this and can make proper attributions in her school newspaper article.

If time allows, student journalists contact the webmaster of the site via e-mail. Most sites provide information about who created the site, when, and how to reach them by e-mail. Students should ask for more details about the basis for what is presented, perhaps including a phone number so a reporter can talk to the source directly.

When using these sites as part of a story or reprinting the information, student journalists have learned not to simply say, "From the Internet." To remain credible, and, in many cases, to avoid breaking copyright laws, student journalists are learning to check and to get an owner's permission. Photos, too, can be part of the entire information package, and generally these belong to the photographer or news agency. It may be easy to download them onto a computer, but it's probably not legal to use them without permission. When writing a paper, a student wouldn't include this entry in the bibliography: "A book in the school library." The Web site's title and/or URL address must be included. Such attention to detail is helping young journalists realize they cannot be lazy when citing information.

Vignette: Getting a Student Newspaper Online

By Candace Perkins Bowen

"Get your newspaper online!" Alief Hastings High School teacher Dianne Smith thinks her colleagues believe she is a bit fanatic about that advice, but she doesn't care. "Tell me: What major daily doesn't have an online edition? In fact, even small dailies and weeklies are taking their information online and with good reason. Internet-savvy people—and that's a huge percentage of the population—seek out information there."

Smith considers herself one of the "old timers," having taken her students from manual typewriters to cumbersome Compugraphic typesetters to Macintosh and PageMaker. "It's simply another step in the technological process," she said of producing for the Web. And it's another way to prepare students for the world beyond the classroom.

Staffs and advisers who want to join the World Wide Web have three main choices. For ease of converting to the Web, some create a portable document format (pdf) file in PageMaker or Adobe Acrobat. This equates to taking a snapshot of the existing print publication and simply posting that. However, a pdf file can't be updated and also lacks the elements that make online publications unique: links to related sites, interactive options like e-mail back to the reporter or reader surveys, and other features such as video clips and sound bites.

The second possibility is creating the Web version from scratch using HTML (hypertext markup language) or using a program like Flash or Dreamweaver. Smith soon realized that putting the Hastings paper, *Bear Facts,* into HTML and completely formatting it for a Web site was quite time-consuming. So she chose a third option. She signed up with one of several free, easy-to-use Web hosting services for scholastic newspapers. The service provided templates, simplified systems to take care of what Smith calls "other housekeeping chores," and easy ways to update the site. In addition, the service adds links to local weather, regional sports and other news, and even possible access to teaching aids such as PBS Online EXTRA and the *New York Times* Learning Network. Whereas other approaches might take weeks, the student webmaster can finish these pages and "go live" with them in a matter of hours.

This doesn't mean Smith's students neglect the basics that have always been part of journalism. They still research, write, and edit dynamic news, features, editorials, and other opinion pieces. And, although the software may be different, they still package the entire piece with eye-catching layouts. Students can customize the hosting service's template colors and make their site look different from other school sites hosted by the same provider.

Smith's students also use the Internet for more than simply displaying the final product. "My staffers do a lot of research on the Net for background info on any in-depth story," she said. "They have found this to be far more satisfactory than searching through archives of magazines and news articles in the library. With nearly every daily newspaper on the Web, the search results are much more thorough and sometimes actually less time-consuming."

Students also seem to spend more time working with the research when they realize how much they can glean from online sources. One topic Hastings reporters covered was identity fraud using social security numbers, a concern because their school required students to wear an ID in school with that number on it. *Bear Facts* staffers found government records, testimony before Senate subcommittees, the text of several laws, and government statistics, in addition to news and feature articles and consumer information. E-mails to daily newspaper reporters, who had written on the subject, and two students in Louisiana, who had led a fight against the same usage in their own school, yielded more angles. Students' research led to more probing questions, and editors pushed back the deadline to allow a chance for further exploration.

Smith's student David Rosen, a sophomore, knows the value of that research. His Web surfing introduced him to the personally intriguing Da Vid, M.D., a third party presidential candidate with the Light Party. From Da Vid's site, Rosen learned more about a man who had run for President not once but three times already. He e-mailed him, expecting no reply, but the candidate called Rosen two hours later. Wanting to get his "exact words instead of relying sheerly on my sloppy notes of him babbling on the phone," Rosen said he asked for an e-mail response to his questions, too.

The resulting article (see the sidebar story below) included a mug shot of Da Vid, downloaded with permission from his Web site, and links to DarkHorse2000, a site reporting on many third party candidates, as well as the Light Party's own site and an article syndicated through Cox News Service with the headline "Reading about the Light Party Makes You Want to Drink a Beer."

Rosen's interview and coverage was not only good enough for *Bear Facts*, it also ran as one of the stories chosen weekly to go up on the *National Edition,* a compilation of top stories from sites hosted by HighWired.net, the hosting service for *Bear Facts*. Jan Prince, *National Edition* editor, said, "When I select stories, I am looking for well-written, entertaining, and informative pieces with a universal appeal to teens and those interested in the youth perspective. The subject does not have to be unique, and many opinion pieces rehash the same topics. But the writing should make the story sound new." Prince, who has used other stories from Rosen, has been impressed not only with his writing but also with his willingness to answer her questions, revise, if necessary, and fill in any holes.

Rosen, a sophomore, has found the whole online experience exhilarating. "Last year," he said, "I finished editing an article at around 3 A.M. my time. I woke up at 6, three hours later, to discover that the story was syndicated in online papers in Belgium, Ohio, and Delaware."

Dark Horse Makes Run for White House as Write-In

Peace, Harmony Themes of Light Party's Standard-Bearer, Da Vid

By David Rosen, Alief (Texas) Hastings High School

With all the media hoopla hovering over the heads of presidential candidates George W. Bush and Al Gore, public attention seems to have left many other contenders in the shadows of silence. Every election year, hundreds of underdogs make a dash for the White House regardless of meager odds. Case in point—Da Vid, M.D.

"I'm every bit as qualified to be President as the candidates from the two main parties," Dr. Vid told the *Bear Facts* in an exclusive interview. "But because of current political trends, people like me aren't allowed in the debates."

Dr. Vid graduated from the University of Miami, Ohio, before going to medical school in Scotland. Shortly after returning to the U.S., he entered the political arena.

"I founded the Human Ecology Party in 1984," Dr. Vid said, "and I officially ran for office in 1992."

Vid also ran unsuccessfully for President in 1996 as a write-in candidate. Regardless of past defeats, however, Vid keeps his sights on the White House.

"Our current focus at this time," Vid said, "is to promote our progressive programs and work with others who support us."

He founded the Light Party in 1993 and has since carried its torch into the Presidential elections. The Light Party's platform includes protecting the environment and preserving personal liberties.

"The foundational work to the Light Party," Vid said, "is that power must be returned to the people."

Vid's past performances have yet to faze him, as he remains faithful in his beliefs. While prominent members of the two major parties may be satisfied with the management of the nation, Vid believes changes need to be made in order to make our Earth a better place.

"Commitment to being a morally sound person is essential now as we are all becoming aware of what needs to be done politically on a local, national and global level," Vid said. "This new age of politics needs to be centered on allowing everyone to live in a society with health, peace and freedom."

Such goals can only be reached through education, Vid believes. Apparently, even the politically active are aware of the importance of a good education.

"Education is the key to everything," Vid said. "We need to emphasize a well-rounded education which emphasizes the arts, ecology and spirituality."

Although his party's platform may seem solid and convincing, Vid's chances for the presidency are rather slim due to the fact that he, along with other third party candidates, isn't allowed to participate in the debates.

"Third parties have as much to offer," Vid said, "in the way of new, progressive ideas, programs and important insights. For instance, Ralph Nader is very aware of the corruption in our present system, and he's just as informed as anyone else."

Along with allowing smaller candidates into the debates, Vid believes the presidential election must be changed in terms of campaign finance. Every election year, according to the Federal Election Commission, millions of dollars are donated to candidates from mega-corporations—stirring conspiracy theories and controversy.

"Until we have campaign finance reform," Vid said, "our system will continue to be inherently and fatally corrupt."

Along with keeping campaign regulation in mind, Vid believes many changes need to be made to the world as a whole. Although somewhat out of the ordinary, his ideas are thought-provoking . . . to say the least.

"Once elected President, the things I'd do," Vid told us, "would be to declare Alcatraz as the Global Peace Center, end the war on drugs and call for an international summit to dismantle all nuclear weapons worldwide."

While his opinions may seem unorthodox or bizarre, Dr. Vid has maintained a strong, firm voice over the years. Bearing an uncanny ability to speak up, Vid will lead his followers into battle with the two-party system in November, and will continue fighting for what he believes in until the day he dies. Dr. Vid, however, doesn't believe his life is anything superhuman. According to him, anyone can make a difference in the world.

"Basically, politics is what happens between people," Vid said, "and thus it's very important to get a good education, be spiritually in touch with yourself and not afraid to speak your opinion."

[This article previously appeared in *Bear Facts*, Alief Hastings High School's online publication, and was reposted on the *National Edition* news digest on HighWired.net.]

Smith Provides Valuable Online Resource

By Candace Perkins Bowen

Dianne Smith helps her students publish online, but she also has a Web presence herself. Her own site, jteacher.com, designed to support journalism teachers and advisers like herself, gets thirty thousand hits a month. "That's absolutely mind-boggling," she said.

The idea was "one of those little seeds that germinates and grows and then totally overtakes the environment," she said. After a devastating misunderstanding with the headmaster at the school where she taught and a series of medical problems, Smith began to write a survival guide for high school journalism teachers "as a form of therapy." She dreamed of getting it published someday, but when the Hastings High School job became hers, the survival guide was "less urgent and relegated to the back burner."

A few years later, more medical problems led to surgery and recuperation at home, where Smith found time to toy with HTML language to translate documents for the Web. "I found my notes for the survival guide, and it hit me I could combine the two ideas," Smith said. At first, it was more of an online classroom "where kids could go for handouts they had missed if they were absent," she said.

Then Smith realized how helpful this might be for journalism teachers. While she knew the major scholastic journalism organizations had Web sites, she thought there was little available for the first-year teacher, a place with exercises, links, ready-to-use help.

Thus she launched *For Journalism Teachers Only*, located at http://www.jteacher.com. It's designed to be "a comprehensive online resource for journalism teachers, publications advisers, and student journalists." Sections include free handouts, downloadable PowerPoint presentations, and information about everything from news to First Amendment issues to digital imaging. Educators like Bobby Hawthorne, author of *The Radical Write*, contributed handouts, and Smith will seek others in the future. Links lead readers to state and national scholastic journalism groups and such news items as an update on how the 1988 Hazelwood Supreme Court decision has affected free expression by students. In addition, a Google search engine allows readers to look for specific topics on the site or on the World Wide Web.

Smith admits that it takes time to maintain the site. She generally spends ten to twenty hours a week updating, looking for new sites to link to, or checking that existing links are still active. But an average of twenty teachers a week e-mail her, excited about what they have found. And, when a technical glitch took some material off the site temporarily, requests from teachers to "please hurry up and get this back" convinced her that what she is doing has been useful. "That couldn't have pleased me more," Smith said.

Standard 9

Students develop an understanding of and respect for diversity in language use, patterns, and dialects across cultures, ethnic groups, geographic regions, and social roles.

Using Journalism

Journalism activities that engage this standard can range widely, from collecting memories and insights of longtime community members—a sort of *Foxfire* publication that captures traditions and heritage—to a much more new-media approach connecting continents. For instance, CUSeeMe desktop videoconferencing allows student journalists to collaborate on stories across town and across the ocean, sharing similarities and differences between their lifestyles and participating in truly collaborative writing.

Vignette: Collaborating with Videoconferencing

By Candace Perkins Bowen

When the Ohio Board of Regents gave grant money to Kent State University to explore the educational value of desktop videoconferencing, some teams joined the group and *then* explored what they might set up as an experiment. Not the group of four high schools and Kent State's School of Journalism and Mass Communication: They already had a plan. The telecommunications hardware and software the grant made available would allow them to connect and collaborate on stories for their student newspapers.

In spring 1999, after one school had to drop out of the project but another enthusiastically joined, they began their first communication. Each school had at least one computer with CUSeeMe software and a microphone and "eyeball" camera attached. At a designated time, participants from each school dialed up the reflector site and "met" with reporters and editors from the other schools. On the computer screen, broken into a grid, they could see each other, and, if the sound was working correctly, they could also hear each other speak. In addition, they could type messages, much like those in an Internet "chat room," which were displayed at the bottom of the screen. Although the frames-per-second rate made this a somewhat jerky visual, the technology was still impressive given the fact that, in some cases, students and teachers were more than one hundred miles apart.

The schools represented a range of sizes and types. One was an inner-ring suburban school with more than twenty-five hundred students and a great deal of diversity. The second was an hour away in a college community. The third represented a small rural area, while the fourth, the last to join the group, was in a blue-collar suburb near another, smaller city. Each had an active, trained adviser and a student-run publication, and the Scholastic Media Program coordinator at Kent State acted as moderator for discussions. A training session for advisers and school technology support personnel took place at the university, and the coordinator set up a listserv through which school personnel could share concerns and announce meeting dates and times.

Initial "meetings" online helped students become more comfortable with the technology and allowed both students and teachers to work out some of the bugs in the system. Early attempts brought problems with sound and color, and with finding a mutually convenient time to talk, but gradually these issues were resolved. By that time, with the help of the moderator, students had begun discussing topics they might like to cover in their school publications. The diversity of the schools made this challenging at first—one staff wasn't interested in problems with Internet filtering, another had just covered a story about the effect of jobs on students and didn't want to do that again, and so on. Some students were not used to covering controversial topics, but others scorned "fluff."

Finally, when a reporter from the rural school mentioned a move in her community to add weighted grades, the enthusiasm grew. "We have it, and it's really not fair," an editor from the large school chimed in. "We don't have anything like that, but I wonder what it's like," added a reporter in the university community. Soon students were discussing the various angles they could cover on the story. What does it mean to have weighted grades? Are there different systems? How do they work? What happens to top students who take classes they want but which aren't weighted? Do the valedictorians have to take fewer classes to stay on top? What do colleges think about such grades? Do they matter?

Before long, students had divided up their topics and started individual research. Several interviewed counselors and students at their schools. One set up an "infographic" chart, indicating the effects on a hypothetical student's grade point average of taking various classes. Another called area college admissions offices, asking how they dealt with the weighted grades. Students set a due date for rough drafts and e-mailed their articles to each other. With those in hand, they met several times via the desktop videoconference setup and discussed ways to improve their work, offering sources at the various schools who might help. They coached each other on the stories, asking questions that might help fill holes that would be confusing to those at other schools.

Although some of the schools had published their last issue too early to include their final work on this story, one school published a five-page "collaborative investigation" in the May 27, 1999 issue. It included articles by its own staffers entitled "Top students have different attitudes about importance of weighted grades, class rank," "Controversy surrounds use, availability of weighted grades," and "AP program has no set grade-weighting criteria." Included, too, were articles from students at the other schools: "KSU changes weighted grades" and "Louisville HS seeks to experiment with weighted grades." Finally, after synthesizing everything and presenting the facts to the readers, the staff wrote an editorial titled, "Drop the H grade; A is reward enough."

In analyzing the project, students all agreed that they enjoyed the process and were surprised at both how similar and how different their schools were. The technology was still a little rough, but students wanted to pursue collaborative writing in the future. An additional reward: The entire package won a "superior" for all eight students at four different high schools in the in-depth category in a statewide writing contest.

Standard 10

Students whose first language is not English make use of their first language to develop competency in the English language arts and to develop understanding of content across the curriculum.

Using Journalism

Journalists realized in the 1970s that their ranks needed to reflect their readers, and that soon those who had been considered minorities would, as a whole, make up the majority. Newsrooms, however, were staffed largely by White, Anglo-Saxon males. The American Society of Newspaper Editors (ASNE), along with a growing number of minority journalists' organizations, began to push for more diversity among those covering the news. For journalists, the bottom line is clear: No longer are professional media concerned with including minorities in their news operations only because of affirmative action guidelines or a sense of being morally right by doing so. Journalists today and tomorrow cannot cover their communities accurately if they don't understand them, and a staff that mirrors the demographics of its community is much more in tune with what is happening than one lacking such diversity.

That continued push has trickled down to secondary schools. In fact, ASNE and other groups have acknowledged that students are more likely to choose journalism as a career if they have participated in it during high school. With this in mind, many organizations support journalism in ethnically diverse areas. Spanish-language newspapers are common, and areas with other strong ethnic populations often encourage student newspapers in their languages. In one community, a student-produced Web page bringing important information to refuges from Kosovo was so popular that similar pages are planned for the future.

But such concerns don't belong only in traditionally diverse urban schools. Preparing all students for the richly varied world they will find after they graduate is a benefit that journalism programs can offer. There are also good opportunities to develop interdisciplinary projects with ESL or foreign-language teachers.

Vignette: Bringing What You Can

By Candace Perkins Bowen

Many of Marian McQuiddy's students don't want to write, even those in her two journalism and two yearbook classes. At Socorro High School near El Paso where she teaches, 98 percent of the twenty-six hundred students are on free lunch and come from lower-income families. Although the district doesn't identify students whose second language is English, she knows many of her students speak Spanish at home.

"We take what they bring to the table and go from there," she said. Lots of samples and "study buddies" are the key, she said.

To produce the two-hundred-page yearbook, she has two classes each semester with, typically, twenty-eight to forty students in each. Students range in age from fourteen to twenty-one. The staff uses a management team approach, not editors, and has ten to twelve managers. "We find a place where everyone can fit," she said.

Those who lack strong English skills pair up with a "buddy," who coaches them in the writing process. Students choose something they want to write about, check out samples with their buddy, sometimes talk their way through the first draft, and eventually begin to polish their copy until it is publishable. McQuiddy said they sell all the books they order each year and do believe they produce something that pleases the other students.

"We find some way so everyone can be successful," she said. Basically, "we do whatever works."

Reaching Out into the Community

By Susan Hathaway Tantillo

An increasing number of students come to our schools whose first language is not English. While administrators and counselors in many schools go to great lengths to explain rules, regulations, and opportunities to these students, most would benefit from having such materials collected in a school handbook written in the students' first language. Such a handbook project would be a wonderful opportunity for pairing more advanced English speakers whose first language is not English with less advanced ones.

More than merely being a translation of an existing school handbook covering rules and regulations, the handbook should also describe student activities, how to get involved in them, and benefits participants have derived from being involved. Students whose first language is not

English should conduct interviews with new students to find out what they want to know. They should also interview students who have been in the school for a year or more to discover what they wish they had known when they were new. They could even interview graduates to find out what they wish they had known, now that they are in college or working.

After all, electronic products today are often packaged with instructions in multiple languages. Schools need to follow suit with their own multilanguage instruction book. Who better to compile it than those who are most affected by it? This would also be a terrific opportunity to pair more advanced students whose first language is not English with less advanced students—to the benefit of both groups.

Students whose first language is not English will learn from formulating the questions to ask, conducting the interviews, finding the answers, organizing and writing each section of the handbook, and overseeing its publication and distribution. Through each step, they will use their own language, develop competency in English language arts, and come to a greater understanding of how all areas of the curriculum work together.

But such a wonderful idea should not be aimed only at students. All too often the parents of students whose first language is not English are forgotten. The handbook's scope should be expanded to include the parent audience. Again, this handbook could be a translation of the school's existing handbook into the parents' first language for distribution to them. Of course, in many of today's schools, this will mean publishing multiple versions of the handbook to accommodate all languages parents speak and read.

As with the student version, an even better option than just translating the existing handbook would be for students to interview parents in their first language to find out what parents do not understand or what they want to know about school rules, and also what they do not understand or what they want to know about the less formal operations or practices of the school. What are some conventional behaviors expected of parents that are not part of the written rules? Ask parents whose first language is not English but who have been around the community for a while what they wish they had known when they first came into contact with the school. What information would have made their lives and their children's lives easier?

Secondary students who successfully publish handbooks for students and/or parents could also lend their skills to middle or elementary schools. Secondary students can act as leaders and facilitators who guide younger students in formulating the questions to ask of their peers and their parents, conducting the interviews, finding the answers to their peers' and parents' questions, and writing the handbook. They may be able to help the younger students publish the final product or they may need to take over the publication on their own and deliver the finished handbooks to the elementary or middle school for distribution.

An ambitious handbook project might even involve selling advertising to merchants in the community to raise the funding necessary for publishing. In this case, students whose first language is not English would need to identify which merchants to approach, design a marketing campaign for contacting the merchants and persuading them to participate, create an advertising contract for merchants to sign and sample ads for inclusion in the handbook, contact the merchants, and follow up with proofs for approval along with bills to assure that the merchants pay per their contract.

In each of these projects, students must practice communication skills using their first language and must process information using critical thinking skills. They create questions, conduct interviews, find the information necessary as a result of the interviews, write summaries of the information they find, and take responsibility for publishing and distributing their product. What better way for students to develop competency in the English language arts (listening, speaking, reading, writing) than by helping their peers and their community simultaneously?

Checking Out the Commercial Press

By Susan Hathaway Tantillo

For this activity, students will need access to stories by professional journalists that have been published in their native language. As an alternative, they might use stories by professional journalists that have been published in a periodical aimed at a specific ethnic group rather than the general population.

A Web search for "foreign language newspapers" yielded 348,000 hits via the Google search engine in January 2002. Going to just the first site listed, that of the Massachusetts Institute of Technology (MIT) Library, resulted in links to Chinese, French, German, Italian, Japanese, Portuguese, Russian, and Spanish electronic journals, newspapers, and magazines. Of course, newspapers not using the English alphabet will require appropriate fonts. The MIT links for Chinese, Japanese, and Russian publications provided further links to obtain the appropriate fonts. Going to the third site listed, the Internet Public Library, uncovered links to a seemingly endless list of newspapers categorized by country, continent, or area of the world and then subdivided. Again, additional fonts would be needed to view foreign language newspapers not using the English alphabet.

Periodicals may also be found in languages other than English by searching Web sites of major metropolitan areas. These searches will also give links to publications written in English but from a particular cultural point of view. For example, in January 2002, the Web site at www.sanjose.com/media offered links to two bilingual newspapers and two Vietnamese newspapers. The site at www.losangeles.com/media gave links to one Russian language newspaper, one Jewish news-and-issues newspaper, one African American community newspaper, and one Pakistani community newspaper, and the site at www.seattle.com/media included links to an Asian American magazine and a Chinese newspaper. Of course, this doesn't work as well with every city, but it is a worthwhile approach.

Besides newspapers from their native language or ethnic group, students will also need common topics if they are going to compare and contrast. The teacher can assign a common topic for exploration, or students can brainstorm topics and decide which one or ones they prefer.

Logical topics for exploration in January 2002 included, but certainly were not limited to, various aspects of the war in Afghanistan, such as the changing roles of women, girls, and education; the conditions in the Guantanamo Bay Naval Base prison holding al-Qaeda and Taliban prisoners; Enron Corporation's bankruptcy and its effect on employees at all levels; ongoing conflicts between Palestinians and Israelis; worldwide airport security measures; and the instability of Argentina's government and banking system.

Topics for exploration are nearly endless and might even include something as frivolous as an analysis of President George W. Bush's fainting spell, attributed to his choking on a pretzel. An article in the *Chicago Tribune* on January 18, 2002, headlined "Foreign media full of theories on Bush's faint," detailed speculations attributed to media in England, France, Italy, Saudi Arabia, Spain, Russia, and Germany. Apparently any news item dealing with the President of the United States gets wide-ranging coverage.

Once students have gathered the stories, they will need to analyze them independently or in small groups where members all look at the same stories. This will help them prepare for group discussion using a common set of criteria and questions, such as:

- name, date, city, and country of publication;
- headlines;
- whether the stories are news, features, or opinion pieces, and how this can be determined;
- whether the stories represent the view of a particular country or a particular ethnic group within the United States, and how;
- what specific sources are used and how they are used/attributed;
- what basic facts are presented;
- what interpretation of facts is presented, if any;
- other criteria that may be included at the discretion of the teacher or students.

Gathering this information will enable students to have an in-depth comparison/contrast discussion of the stories they have found. Once they have shared their findings, students will be able to draw conclusions about how journalists in different countries or from different ethnic groups in the United States cover the same news event and whether these journalists seem to be biased.

Vignette: *Expresión Juvenil*, a Spanish Newspaper That Started as a Class Project

By Eugenia Sarmiento Lotero

I have been a teacher in urban schools where the Hispanic population is the majority. Presently, I am teaching at Abraham Lincoln High School in Denver. The classes I teach are geared to help students coming from Mexico acquire better skills in their native language so they can transfer those skills to the learning of English.

There are four levels of Spanish language classes. The first level is Spanish for Spanish Speakers, which addresses below-grade-level reading and writing skills in the native language. Spanish Reading Composition is the second level. Its curriculum is literature-based and can help students successfully take the Introduction to English Literature course required in order to graduate from the Denver Public Schools (DPS). The other two courses are more advanced: Spanish AP Language and Spanish AP Literature, where students are in a more rigorous setting being prepared to take the national AP tests.

I have been very lucky to have the most incredible students in my classes. Unfortunately, many of my colleagues miss the opportunity to enjoy having high-level thinking activities in class when teaching second-language learners due to the language barrier. Many times, students' intelligence has been insulted when a teacher gives them activities for elementary levels under the assumption that they cannot accomplish anything higher.

This was one of the reasons my students and I wanted to do a project to make my students proud of themselves and of their culture. The Spanish AP Language class was in charge of directing the newspaper, and we invited other classes to contribute articles. Posters were displayed around the school in Spanish, inviting every Spanish speaker to participate. For two months, announcements were given every morning through the intercom encouraging every Spanish-speaking student to participate.

I called local newspapers to request their help in publishing the paper, but many newspapers were not ready at that time to support us. Finally, through *La Voz*, a local newspaper, we were put in contact with Valentina Garcia. She taught the students how to organize a paper and how to obtain reports and interviews, and, more important, she developed a very strong relationship with my students.

One afternoon, in April, several candidates for the superintendent position at DPS came to Lincoln to meet with the community and answer their questions. Two of my strong reporters covered this news and they asked those candidates excellent questions about their position on bilingual education. Local media representatives were there, and the *Rocky Mountain News* called me later to see what we were doing.

From there, everything took off. Channel 50 (part of the Spanish-language Univision Network) did a special report on the project and the class. Later, a local Fox TV news crew also did a report. As a result, we established a legacy in the community. Valentina Garcia put us in contact with Saint Anthony's hospital. They donated $500, and she also put us in contact with the printing company where her paper was printed.

Many talents were discovered through this project. Alma García, who was in charge of the design, created a very attractive layout. Ramiro Arenivar and Miguel Rodríguez explored and became experts at using Adobe PageMaker. Others improved their Spanish skills by proofreading and editing the paper. Alma, upon her graduation, will pursue a career in media. Presently, she is the designer of the second edition of the newspaper, and even though she is not enrolled in the AP class, she became my assistant to support this edition.

Today, my Spanish AP Language class has continued the legacy of the project. The class also wants to improve the paper. Students like

Martha Olivas, Perla Manquero, José Pérez, Francisco Morales, and others are determined to make this edition as successful as the last one or even better.

As I expressed to all the reporters before with great pride: this started as a class project, and it was never intended to compete with the school newspaper. It met a need for us to be able to express our opinions, points of view, and feelings in our own language. We wanted to show the community the creativity and the leadership abilities of the Hispanic students and how well versed they are in subjects such as literature, art, and science. My students read novels that are well beyond people's expectations for these students, by authors such as Miguel de Unamuno, Federico García Lorca, Paulo Coehlo, and José Saramago. We were very proud of our cultural background, and it was well received.

One of the advantages that I have found with this project is the fact that students implement their writing skills not only in preparing their own articles but also in proofreading and editing articles submitted by other students. They learn editing procedures they can then apply in English, a language transfer skill that would be helpful in their bilingual settings.

After the completion of the first edition, we received letters from West High School and other institutions congratulating us for a job well done. Students were so proud of their paper that after the distribution of *Expresión Juvenil*, one could not find a paper in a trash can or left on desks as usually happens after students read the school newspaper. The articles utilized a universal genre—that is, they were framed so they would be relevant over time, not just on the day of publication—and parents wanted to keep a copy for future reference, especially the articles such as one on the drug Ecstasy and another titled "De hijos a padres" ("from children to parents").

All in all, this has not been my success. It has been the success of members of a culture working together, of a community that needed to be recognized and appreciated for its contributions not only to the educational arena but also to the media itself. I want to thank all of those who made this possible, but especially my beautiful students, whom I love with all my heart.

Standard 11

Students participate as knowledgeable, reflective, creative, and critical members of a variety of literacy communities.

Using Journalism

Seamless education is broadening the literacy communities students can easily access. Nowhere is that more evident than in journalism. Citywide and community newspapers actively recruit teen writers for their pages, knowing that tomorrow's newspaper readers must get their start now. Publishers want to entice teen readers with topics that interest them, written by people they recognize as friends in math or science class, and newspapers often do this by offering help to the school's journalism teacher. Students have also embraced the cyber community as their own. Through a slowly growing number of online journalism classes and through Internet work in more traditional journalism classes, students are connecting to communities all around the world. With support from their teachers, they are accessing information and sharing their views through interactive Web sites and their own homepages.

Vignette: Understanding a Web Audience

By Candace Perkins Bowen with Christine Kaldahl

Plenty of professional journalists work on daily newspapers and Web sites updated hourly or even more often. But student media vehicles generally come out weekly at best; most publications, in fact, are monthly. So when Millard South High School adviser Christine Kaldahl's husband suggested a daily online story, the idea clicked. "The practice of producing something daily was simply exciting to us," she said.

The online *Daily Citizen* was launched as an extension of the existing print newspaper she already advised in an Omaha suburb. One of the fifteen students is editor in chief of the site and manages the copy flow, weekly and monthly assignment board, site design, and related details. An assistant editor helps with site design, site maintenance, and copyediting. The staff meets daily, for elective credit, and posts a new story and photo by noon on each day that school is in session.

The staff holds brainstorming sessions to find story topics but also utilizes a calendar listing school events, board meetings, and special days. "Anytime we see a 'National _____ Day,' we write it on the calendar," Kaldahl said. "Sometimes serious, sometimes wacky, these special days give us a starting point for ideas." For instance, during National School Lunch Week, the staff has planned personality profiles of cafeteria workers, a nutrition story, and a "review" of typical school lunch specials. While they know their audience is broader than that of the school's print newspaper, they generally keep most stories "school-based."

The Web site runs more timely stories than the print version can—QuickTime video of Tuesday's varsity softball game runs that same week—but it can't offer the same depth. When students covered a board meeting, the online story two days later showed only one aspect—a report on Advanced Placement classes and how many students take them. By the time the print version was out several weeks later, the reporter had interviewed the principal in charge of generating that report, who went over the significance of the some of the statistics and what the differences between the three high schools in the district might mean. The reporter also interviewed a representative from a college that offers credit for courses taught in the high school building. "There was more meat in the print version and more timeliness in the online," Kaldahl said.

> *Our school is moving from a seven-period day to an eight-period alternating block schedule next year. For at least two years, this pending scheduling change has been highly debated. The principal announced at a faculty meeting after school on October 3 what the new schedule would be. Another meeting was held on the morning of October 4 to accommodate all the teachers who could not attend on the first day.*
>
> *On Friday, October 5, we ran the following story. This is exactly the kind of story I was hoping to be able to do with our Web site. This highly debated topic was something everyone wanted to know about, and we were able to run the story in a timely manner. The student reporter had attended a parent forum on the scheduling issue a week earlier and saw the principal's presentation, enabling her to have much of the background work and an interview with the principal completed before the announcement was made.*
>
> *Here is her story.*
>
> —Adviser Christine Kaldahl

Principal Announces Block Scheduling

By Sarah Swedberg, Millard South High School, Omaha, Nebraska

Principal Dr. Dick Wollman announced on Oct. 4 that next year Millard South will be on an alternating block schedule. He stated several reasons for changing from the traditional seven-period schedule to the alternating block schedule. These reasons include the increase in graduation requirements, creating more opportunities to take more courses, to maintain/increase elective opportunities, to increase student achievement, to reduce daily hectic pace, and to reduce discipline infractions.

Social Studies teacher Pam Norlen said that she thinks the main reason why Wollman is changing the schedule is because as the number of credits to graduate increases, students need to have the option to take more classes.

Originally the eight-period modified schedule was being considered, until Wollman decided to postpone implementation due to facility renovation, issues impacting staff, increased graduation requirements that were being considered, and district staffing support.

"Originally (MS) planned to implement a new schedule in the fall of 2000, but announced a year ago to postpone (the decision)," Wollman said. "A decision I have not regretted."

However, some teachers say they would have preferred the eight-period modified schedule.

"If I was to pick, it would be the eight-period modified schedule because I like to see my kids every day, and that's the closest schedule to it," math teacher Ken Hui said.

Wollman looked at the four-by-four block schedule, but because of the eight- to twelve-month gap between sequenced courses such as math and foreign language it was turned down.

"My preference probably would have been the straight (four by four) block, but according to research it appears it may not be as good for the students," Norlen said.

On the alternating block schedule, students will have four classes one day and a different four classes the next. Some advantages of having this scheduling would be a less hectic class schedule

> for students and staff (with more homework opportunities and nights available), lessened sequenced course gap between grades and standardized achievement tests, and teacher planning time is longer on one day.
>
> Chemistry Teacher Cece Schwennsen said that an alternating block schedule would reduce the number of times a teacher has to repeat things in a day.
>
> "I teach an advanced placement class, and this schedule would allow the maximum amount of time an AP kid would be in my class before the AP exam," Schwennsen said.

Vignette: Reaching Across the Ocean

By Candace Perkins Bowen

When publication adviser Shirley Yaskin spent three summers in Eastern Europe teaching "fact-based" journalism to high school students in Hungary and Romania, she brought home more than memories. The Miami Palmetto Senior High teacher was one of six trainers who took part in the program, sponsored by the Independent Journalism Foundation of New York in 1998, with additional workshops in 1999 and 2000. But her connections with her overseas students didn't end when she flew home at the end of each workshop.

Sorana Ester, one of the teenage workshop participants from Bucharest, flew to Florida to visit Yaskin and her staff in August 1998, applying what she had learned to help them put out the first issue that year. She stayed with then-junior and *Panther* Focus editor Jamie Kleinerman, forming a special bond. (The online version of the newspaper can be viewed by clicking the appropriate link on the school's Web site at http://www.dade.k12.fl.us/palmetto/.)

"Her joy and enthusiasm in the newsroom was unparalleled, as she actively participated in discussions on potential articles and asked to design pages," Jamie wrote in an article for *Quill & Scroll* magazine (Kleinerman 2000, 6). Jamie also discovered that Sorana and her friends wanted to develop contacts with teenagers in the United States, in part so "they could learn about growing up in democratic America." Soon the Miami students had cyber pen pals halfway around the world.

The pen pals also made good news sources. When *Panther* staff members did an in-depth, multi-article spread about the fighting in

Kosovo in its April 22, 1999, issue, they were able to include insight from teenagers much closer to the problem.

"The Kosovo situation has a great impact (economically and socially) on all countries in Yugoslavia's neighborhood," Sorana wrote. "Sometimes I feel unsafe and I am worried that this war will spread through Romania. I was with my boyfriend, walking in the park in Bucharest, and I almost cried while looking at some kids playing because their future is unclear and some could be orphans."

Anna Kutor wrote, "In Hungary, people down by the south border can hear the bombing and they are very frightened. People say this war will be longer than the one in Vietnam. All they can talk about in the news here is the war. People hope it does not spread to Hungary."

In an article by guest writer Martin Munz, the Hungarian student explained, "I'm a 17-year-old high school student, and I have a lot of dreams and plans about my future. I'd like to go to university, and after it I'd like to study abroad. Some weeks ago I got a letter from the military. All of my friends got that same letter. They want us to go in for conscription."

Jamie also found out that Romanian and Hungarian schools don't offer journalism courses, even though some of the students want to pursue that career.

"Because of this, I decided to start chapters of Quill and Scroll, an international organization for student journalists, in these countries," she said. The chance to have such a link with other student journalists around the world "excited the students in Romania and Hungary," Jamie said. But they still had a major hurdle: The $40 charter fee and $11.50 each for dues were too much for either the schools or the students to pay.

So Jamie went to work.

Miami-area businesses contributed to Jamie's cause, and the U.S. pen pals not only wrote—and continue to write—to their overseas friends, but they also paid their membership dues.

Jamie's dream was realized when Yaskin and fellow trainer Merle Dieleman inducted sixteen members into a Quill and Scroll chapter at the Center for Independent Journalism in Bucharest during summer 2000. Although the group received its charter as the first Eastern European chapter the December before, the students delayed the official ceremony until the Americans arrived for the summer workshop.

As Yaskin wrote in *Quill & Scroll* magazine, "When Merle brought out the big blue-and-gold Quill and Scroll banner, the students thought it was beautiful. There were candles and a portion of the traditional ceremony encouraging the students to seek the truth in their quest as journalists.

"Each was called forward to receive the traditional Quill and Scroll pin and membership card," all made possible by Jamie and members of Miami Palmetto's Quill and Scroll chapter.

Less than a year later, on March 15, 2000, twenty-five students and three faculty members were inducted when Quill and Scroll executive director Dick Johns conducted a second ceremony in Budapest, Hungary. Johns, of Hungarian descent, reacted to the experience with surprise and joy. "The surprise part is due to the previous environment in which these teenagers and their parents had lived prior to the fall of the Berlin Wall and the Iron Curtain. Now the seeds of democracy were beginning to take root, but not without some fear and reservation about the longevity of their independence."

The students, Johns said, meet once each week to develop the skills of researching, interviewing, writing, editing, and design and to publish a magazine in both English and Hungarian.

"These young people are the hope and future of democracy in their country, and investing in their knowledge and experience about freedom of the press and freedom of speech is so critical," Johns said.

Yaskin and students in the journalism program at Miami Palmetto High School agree. "I still exchange letters with Michael from Romania," said Yaskin, "and he summarized our experiences best when he said, 'I love talking with you through letters and e-mails! I have so many questions that I can't wait to ask you and look forward to our many chats in the future.'"

Work Cited

Kleinerman, Jamie. 2000. "Kleinerman Helps to Establish New Charters in Hungary, Romania." *Quill & Scroll* (February/March): 6.

Standard 12

Students use spoken, written, and visual language to accomplish their own purposes (e.g., for learning, enjoyment, persuasion, and the exchange of information).

Using Journalism

As long as student media are indeed that—organized with students as the decision makers—journalism provides a valuable way for them to accomplish Standard 12. As editors, reporters, and designers for their school newspapers, magazines, yearbooks, online publications, and broadcast outlets, they must produce something for an audience. They are responsible for deciding (or finding out) what the audience wants and needs to know, and for doing the research—the reporting—to get the facts. To those elements, they add entertainment, with a variety of features, and persuasion, with editorials, reviews, columns, cartoons, and advertising. Their peer coaching and editing ensures that the work follows journalistic and other conventions, and designers package it all for an audience. Each product represents student voices and is created by students using skills they have learned from interacting with teachers/advisers and following professional models they have read and viewed. Some of their stories carry them beyond their school grounds, when they have the opportunity to make a difference to the community.

Vignette: Mentoring Future Journalists

By Candace Perkins Bowen

Chris Tracy was a student himself, a senior at Davenport (Iowa) Central High School, when he became head organizer of a journalism workshop for third- through fifth-grade students. And he learned an important lesson:

"Learning in school is usually boring, and the kids' attention spans are not very wide when they are that young. This is why we have to make the kids think they aren't learning when they really are. Journalism can provide this kind of teaching."

Tracy was part of the All Cultural Achievement Plan (which began in 1996–97) and its ten-day Summer Journalism Academy. The idea of Davenport teacher Deb Buttleman Malcolm, the Academy has been student-driven since the start. Students who have taken Malcolm's journalistic writing course are the organizers and teachers, focusing on the skills they have learned in their class and on the staff of the school's *BlackhawK* newspaper. Some of Malcolm's former students, like Tracy, even return from college to continue their participation.

Their goals for their young students range from introducing the importance of reading and writing to the minority students they work with to encouraging them to consider college careers—perhaps even in journalism. "We set out to make literacy a priority in the lives of children and instill a liking for reading and writing," said junior Mariah Pearl Cunnick, a co-coordinator of the 2000–01 activities.

Each of the nearly sixty grade-school students in the summer 2000 program rotated through instruction and activities on a variety of journalistic skills: reporting and basic interviewing, writing, photography, videography. Their teen teachers, all state or national award winners for their own publications work, took in-service with Malcolm and used a series of handouts she developed. They also used their class notes and experiences. "The other key," Malcolm said, "was each student taught his or her specialty area—thus learning more about it by having to explain it each day as a new group of young students rotated [into the class]."

The final product—a group newspaper—came about after students had studied all the basics and had taken field trips to the University of Iowa, the *Quad-City Times,* and Pioneer Village, a nearby cluster of historic buildings from the later 1800s. Using a team approach, they applied what they had learned.

That wasn't always easy. Breaking students into smaller groups was a plus because, as Tracy said, the most difficult part of teaching was trying to keep all of them working at the same time. "Sometimes they were more worried about getting an extra cookie rather than writing a good news story," sophomore Manuel Garcia said.

The results, however, were impressive. The thirty-page newsmagazine includes articles about the Summer Journalism Academy in general; interviews with reporters, artists, and editors at the *Times*; reports on their trip to the university; descriptions of the Buffalo Bill Cody Homestead and of Pioneer Village; and interviews with Native Americans. Each article has at least one photo, as well as sidebars to give additional information.

Who learned more—the grade school students or their teen teachers? It's hard to say. Tracy was pleased when a student she had worked with for two years in the Academy signed a contract stating that he would earn straight A's if he could be the student video producer at the upcoming Academy. Senior Kris Cooks was impressed with the progress returning students had made. Cunnick added, "We succeeded with our short-term goals of producing a publication and having fun while learning and improving their skills. But long-term goals cannot yet be imagined if they share their learning with others or it improves their own quality of life."

Malcolm saw changes in her students, who also did case studies of "their little learners."

"I saw them grow as leaders and in critical thinking skills as they worked with the younger students. Now, when we have editorial board problems [on their student publication], they speak out almost as mother/father figures and are not afraid to question peer judgment," Malcolm said.

Cunnick agreed. "I have come from a home where reading, writing and education have been *very* stressed. I learned here that if kids can be taught this importance early on, not only will it help them their entire lives, but it will be carried on. I also learned on a personal level more leadership and the ability to more easily 'take charge.' That carries over into our newspaper and my life in general. Somebody has to speak up and get things done. We all got a lot of practice with those kids! And we all got a big dose of patience along the way!"

Local Native American Talks about Indian Heritage

By T. J. Pearson, Summer Journalism Academy, Davenport (Iowa) Central High School

Les Miller, a local Native American, came to the ACAP Journalism Academy at Central High School to explain his culture.

"I live a modern life," Miller said.

Even though he does live a modern life, he is very connected to his culture. Five years ago, to become more connected to his Indian heritage, he started Wednesday night pow-wows with his fellow Indian friends.

"To us, the earth is Grandmother, and nature is Grandfather. They are very sacred to us."

He told the story of Crazy Horse and talked about the monument that is being carved out of a mountain in South Dakota.

> "Crazy Horse predicted that he would be known around the world, and now he is. Millions of people can see him now," Miller said.
> Miller also told of a story about a little Indian boy and a rattlesnake. The little boy heard a cry of help from a pit near a mountain. It was a rattlesnake, who kept asking him for help. The little boy knew that the snake would bite him, but the snake swore he wouldn't.
> The boy eventually rescued him from the pit and took him near the mountain. The snake bit him soon after, and when the boy asked, "Why did you bite me? You said you wouldn't." The snake replied, "You knew I would bite you. You knew."
> Miller told the students the moral of the story was to stay away from drugs and alcohol because "it will bite you."

Vignette: Reporting on the Community

By Candace Perkins Bowen

"When I began writing this story, it was just another regular news event that had to be covered, only the topic was more touchy, since it dealt with a death." Thus Iliana Montauk, a junior on the Berkeley (California) High School *Jacket* newspaper, began helping her fellow staffer, Megan Greenwell, plug up some holes in a story Greenwell had worked on for a week. Greenwell had asked for her help to "back up information with more quotes, find any problems with libel," and conduct even more interviews. Greenwell knew the story was important, but neither student journalist realized it would soon become one of national significance. Soon Greenwell and Montauk became the news themselves as they discovered immigrants from India laboring in indentured servitude in their community.

As part of her daily Journalism 2 class, Greenwell decided to investigate a carbon monoxide poisoning that had occurred in a local apartment building over Thanksgiving break. What struck her and her teacher Rick Ayers as strange was the fact that the woman was seventeen years old, yet no one in the school seemed to know her. Then the news staff heard rumors of a slave ring in the area. Montauk assigned the story to Greenwell, but when it grew into more than an obituary—although not a story about a slave ring—and because deadline was only a week and a half away, Montauk worked on it as well.

"The story was something there for anyone to get . . . only the 'professional' journalists did not bother. They checked out that the death was an accident, and that was enough," Ayers said.

Those interviewed included Dharini Rasiah, video teacher at the school; Hina Shah, an attorney for the Asian Law Caucus in San Francisco; a spokesperson at the electric company; two students at the University of California, Berkeley; and one student at the high school itself. Others who were interviewed wished to remain anonymous.

Ayers said their investigative reporting was just like all reporting of that type. "It was a matter of having contacts. They could talk to Indian and other South Asian students they knew through ESL [English as a Second Language class]. They could talk to South Asian teachers at Berkeley High," he explained. He said many of the students were afraid to talk and would not have talked to a *San Francisco Chronicle* reporter, but they would talk to the young women on the condition of anonymity.

Montauk agreed. "Our age helped a lot. Many people felt less threatened because we were young and because we weren't writing for a professional paper. Some said things similar to 'What's this for? Just your high school newspaper? Okay, I can talk to you.'"

She also believes some of the young adults talked to them because they thought they would listen and understand. "We were curious," she said. "And we weren't doing it because our paper needed to blow it up on the front page. . . . We were just writing the story we found; we hadn't been searching for a cover story."

With their information in order, they wrote the article. That wasn't easy either, even though they had good sources. Ayers noted the struggle to avoid an anti-Indian-immigration story or a "sex slave sensational story." He also helped the reporters see that Vijay Reddy, owner of the apartment building, was "not just the bad guy here."

"He is just a creation, a typical creation, of a world economy with such great haves and have-nots. The students got that, not right away but over the course of the discussions," Ayers said.

Once the paper came out, the media latched onto it and began focusing on the high school publication and Montauk and Greenwell. "The most we learned from this experience took place a month after we wrote the article, once the media started paying attention to us," Montauk said. It showed them the "real world of journalism," and they were sometimes excited, sometimes disappointed. The experience gave impetus for ethics discussions on their staff.

Highlights included an invitation to visit National Public Radio while in Washington, D.C., on a class trip. "It was interesting seeing 'All Things Considered' being created, and meeting the people whose voices I had heard on the radio, and who worked behind the scenes," Montauk said.

There were low points, too. The girls said some information about them was inaccurate and even blatantly false. For example, some newspapers wrote that they had discovered a "prostitution ring" in Berkeley. Also, some of the people they talked to were impolite and disrespectful. "We felt that they treated us like children. When we refused interviews [because they were overwhelmed by the number of requests], they could not understand why. . . . They seemed to think that it was everyone's dream to be in their magazines. Some were insistent and rude."

"The diversity of Berkeley High School served a purpose," Ayers said. "It was a chance to have the information cross over from one community to the next, to get help and support for a group that was being terribly exploited."

Montauk knows the media attention made a difference in her life. "It's not normal for a person my age to be getting requests for interviews with *People* magazine and to be bargaining with TV movie production companies," she said. She also learned "how people we interview might feel and why they might be angry when they see their story in print, even though we may think we got all the information right."

But did it make a difference in the community and the future of immigrants in the area? Montauk modestly said she is not an expert on the issue. "Reddy's arrest by the police and [Immigration and Naturalization Service] probably made a bigger difference," she said.

Greenwell believes the story helped her grow as a writer. Since it came during her first semester on the *Jacket*, she was a fairly inexperienced writer. Although she admits she was "kind of winging it," since she had never written this type of investigative piece, she believes it made her a better writer. "It was an article that got me thinking. Because it was such a sensitive issue, I had to take everything into account. There were libel issues to consider, as well as cultural boundaries and anonymity. Now I feel like I am better equipped to deal with those types of things," she said.

But Greenwell also looks philosophically at the experience. "Usually news articles are quickly forgotten in a period of a few days, but it is through the media that the general public gets all their information. Think about what you know about George W. Bush. Assuming you don't know him personally, everything you know and think about him is from a newspaper article or story on the news. So when the media misses such a big story, the public just doesn't know.

"That's the responsibility of good reporters. You can't miss anything. So, in the big picture, our story was significant because it uncovered something that everyone else, including the police, missed. That, for me, is what makes the story worth it. It's not the fame or the recognition that gives the story value. Although it took a death before the issue could come to light, the fact that it did come up potentially saved more lives."

Young Indian Immigrant Dies in Berkeley Apartment

South Asian Community Says 'Indentured Servitude' May Be to Blame

By Megan Greenwell and Iliana Montauk, *The Jacket*, Berkeley (California) High School

The recent death of a young Indian immigrant girl in a Berkeley apartment has brought up deep issues about the exploitation of young workers.

Seetha Vemireddy, 17, died after a blocked heating vent in the apartment she shared with her sister filled their room with highly poisonous carbon monoxide. Her sister was taken to Alta Bates Hospital in critical condition, and has since been released.

Residents of 27 other apartments in the Berkeley Park Apartments were evacuated to a nearby hotel after the defective heating units were discovered. "The heaters tested at 2,000 parts per million of carbon monoxide," explained Jonathan Franks, a PG&E [Pacific Gas & Electric] spokesperson. "The sensitivity device only goes up to 2,000, so it seems likely it was higher."

The building's owner, Vijay Reddy, owns many of Berkeley's largest apartment buildings, along with Pasand restaurant and one hotel.

Seetha Vemireddy, though high-school aged, was not attending Berkeley High or any other Bay Area high school, according to a BHS student who knew her but wished to remain anonymous.

Many of the youth whom the *Jacket* contacted asked to remain anonymous. Some insinuated that they feared for their safety.

"Se wasn't going to school," the student continued. "Se was just working for Mr. Reddy, at his restaurant and the apartments."

Several members of the South Asian community have speculated that Vemireddy was probably an "indentured servant." Indentured servitude means that an employer in the United States helps bring foreigners over, possibly paying for their visas and their passage, and then requires that the immigrants work for low pay, sometimes below minimum wage.

"People can bring their family over to work," the same student said. "[The employers] usually provide them with food, shelter, all the basics, but the employees aren't paid much, if at all. I know that Vijay Reddy sets up contracts for people to come to the U.S. and work. Seetha probably came through him."

That speculation has remained unconfirmed, although it has been established that Vemireddy was working instead of attending school.

Although indentured servitude is illegal, it can exist because employers can help bring people from foreign countries to the U.S. by sponsoring them for work visas. "The employer has to show that there is a lack of people in the U.S. with the skills needed to do the job," said Hina Shah, lawyer for the Asian Law Caucus.

UC Berkeley student Mukti Chamitiganti said that it is commonly known in the Indian community that indentured servitude exists in restaurants in the area. A UCB sophomore who preferred to remain anonymous also said that she had been told not to eat at Pasand because the workers there were exploited.

Berkeley High video teacher Dharini Rasiah said that exploitation of Indians who come on an indentured servitude basis can happen for many reasons. She said that such immigrants are vulnerable because they do not have the skills necessary to find another job, because they do not speak English, and because they feel indebted to their employers.

"Workers are almost under care of their employer and there's a sense of obligation from workers to employers," said Rasiah. "There's a sense of debt and it's hard to break out of that."

Although the Indian community seems to be aware of this issue, many people said that indentured servitude is often seen as

▶

an opportunity for Indians. Rasiah said that the term "indentured servitude" is not used in the community. "That sounds like a negative thing. [Some people think] it's a positive thing because people are bringing people over who wouldn't be able to come. Someone's bringing them over and giving them a life that could be better than in India."

Chamitiganti said, "Since we're looking at it from an American viewpoint, it seems negative, but it all depends on perspective." She added that if people in India were told of the situation for workers here, they would think it was normal.

Rasiah, Chamitiganti, and a few youth who preferred to remain anonymous said that people think of indentured servitude as a community issue. However, both Rasiah and Shah are involved in a collaboration with lawyers and activists whose goal is to "look at the needs of the South Asian community" including worker exploitation, according to Shah. Shah said that, if she were to hear specific allegations involving indentured servitude, she would be very interested in investigating the case. Although she has received several phone calls reporting rumors of exploitation in Indian restaurants in Berkeley and Mountain View, no specific allegations with concrete evidence have been made.

"There's a great fear to speak out because workers are afraid of being retaliated against from their employer," said Shah. She also mentioned that if anyone would be willing to give her more information, she could be contacted at (415) 391-1655.

Conclusion

Do exercises and experiences in the world of journalism help students develop the skills and capacities that the NCTE/IRA standards suggest they should develop? Definitely. In a very real-world setting, students pursuing these activities in a journalism class or as a unit in an English or language arts class must read print and nonprint texts to learn about themselves and the world around them. They gather information about society from newspapers and television, from the World Wide Web and from radio. This, after all, is where they will gain most of their knowledge after they leave school, and the critical eye and ear they develop in the classroom will carry their learning into the future.

Through what they write as reporters and editors, they respond to society's needs: They offer suggestions for ways to improve school security and become active in community issues; they combat their readers' stress or suggest they take a break with a good movie. To really understand these readers' needs, they must tap into the human experience. For they know, as journalists, they must write for their audience. To do this, they must become observers, readers, listeners. And once they know what their audience needs, they must apply a wide range of journalistic strategies to convey the message. Should it be an in-depth article? An information graphic? A visual package with photos, text, and bullet-pointed fact boxes? Audio? Video? In today's multimedia world, the possibilities are endless. And student journalists are weighing the pros and cons of all those possibilities.

These varied methods of communicating also allow students to access more expert sources, to collaborate with other writers, and to reach a wider audience, perhaps even halfway around the world. Lawyers and doctors, educators and librarians, those with unique and interesting facts to help the young journalists tell their stories and offer vital information to their readers—all are relatively easy to access in the digital world. Logging on to their Web sites, connecting through e-mail, and following up with a telephone interview are just some of the new methods. These all allow today's student journalists to print or broadcast more than the "same old same old" articles about student council meetings and the next sporting event. They can provide readers with information they can use.

In addition, more and more journalists are learning to share the research and writing process with other writers across the city, the state, or the world. Collaboration through e-mail and videoconferencing allows them to discover the striking similarities and differences between themselves and their peers elsewhere, and they can offer that perspective to their readers and viewers. In the process, they also learn to value their diversity and view it as an asset to their learning.

And with this knowledge of the world around them and of themselves, student journalists of all ages can grow and learn and make a difference. That, after all, is what the twelve NCTE/IRA standards are about, and what any good teacher wants to achieve.

Authors

Candace Perkins Bowen, Master Journalism Educator (MJE), is Scholastic Media Program coordinator for Kent State University's School of Journalism and Mass Communication. After more than twenty years of advising award-winning high school newspapers and yearbooks in Illinois and Virginia, she came to Ohio to develop this program in June 1995. Although Kent State had supported a high school press association for sixty years, it has now developed a more thorough approach, with summer and weekend workshops, connections with the College of Education, and outreach to area schools. The immediate past president of the Journalism Education Association, Bowen manages that group's listserv and realizes just how important it is for advisers to have solid information and a network of support. She is currently head of the Council of Affiliates for the Association for Education in Journalism and Mass Communication, working to be sure that those in commercial media support school programs. She also serves on the board of the Student Press Law Center. Her honors include National High School Journalism Teacher of the Year from the Dow Jones Newspaper Fund, the Carl Towley and Medal of Merit Awards from the Journalism Education Association, the Pioneer Award from the National Scholastic Press Association, and the Gold Key from the Columbia Scholastic Press Association.

Susan Hathaway Tantillo, Master Journalism Educator (MJE), taught journalism and English and advised the student newspaper, *Spokesman*, from 1971 to 2001 at Wheeling (Illinois) High School (WHS). She is coauthor of the high school journalism textbook *Introduction to Journalism* (2001). Her educational background includes a B.A. in English from Purdue University (1967) and an M.A. in journalism from Indiana University (1969). She was the first Teacher of the Year at WHS. Throughout her thirty-year career in education, Tantillo spoke frequently at state, regional, and national high school press days and conventions, and she served on the board of directors of the Journalism Education Association (JEA) from 1978 until retirement. Currently, she judges for state and national journalism organizations. During her tenure as *Spokesman* adviser, her students received 489 individual writing, photography, and design awards from state, regional, and national organizations, including nineteen Quill and Scroll National Writing Awards. Tantillo's personal honors include JEA's Carl Towley, Lifetime Achievement, and Medal of Merit Awards; the National Scholastic Press Association's Pioneer and All-American Adviser Awards; the Columbia Scholastic Press Association's Gold Key Award; and the Kettle Moraine Press Association's Hall of Fame and Adviser of the Year Awards.

Contributors

Note: CJE *indicates Certified Journalism Educator, a designation teachers can earn from the Journalism Education Association (JEA) through a combination of course work, classroom experience, and/or written test.* MJE *indicates Master Journalism Educator, another JEA designation, based on additional years in the classroom, a required essay test, and a journalism-related project.*

John Bowen, MJE, is in his thirty-first year as a journalism and social studies teacher and publications adviser at Lakewood (Ohio) High School. Since 1982 he has also taught prospective journalism teachers at Kent State University. Among Bowen's teaching honors are the 1983 Dow Jones Newspaper Fund National Journalism Teacher of the Year, the Journalism Education Association's Carl Towley Award, the Pioneer Award from the National Scholastic Press Association, and the Gold Key from the Columbia Scholastic Press Association. In 2001 he received the Distinguished Service Award from the Cleveland chapter of the Society of Professional Journalists (SPJ). His professional involvement includes serving on the board of directors of the Student Press Law Center, as chairman of JEA's Scholastic Press Rights Commission, and as an instructor/speaker at local, regional, and national journalism workshops, seminars, and conventions. Bowen's publication achievements include having ten SPJ student scholarship winners and five JEA National High School Journalist of the Year winners or runners-up.

Michele Dunaway, MJE, is a high school English teacher with more than fourteen years in education. She has served on the boards of the Sponsors of School Publications of Greater St. Louis, the Missouri Interscholastic Press Association, and the Journalism Education Association (JEA). Besides having authored three professional articles for *Communication: Journalism Education Today,* Dunaway also compiled JEA's current Middle/Junior High Journalism Curriculum guide, including authoring sections of the document. In addition to presenting workshops at national and regional conventions, Dunaway has also served as a textbook reviewer for NTC/Contemporary and writes contemporary series romance for Harlequin American Romance. She has published four books, with upcoming releases in progress.

Lisa O. Greeves has taught English and journalism courses at Thomas Jefferson High School for Science and Technology in Alexandria, Virginia, and at Rockbridge County High School in Lexington, Virginia. She has worked both with technical preparation students and with students designated as gifted and talented. She holds a bachelor's degree in English and journalism from James Madison

University and a master's degree in English with a concentration in writing and rhetoric from Virginia Commonwealth University. She tries to create writing assignments that incorporate technology and the Internet in realistic, practical ways.

H. L. Hall, MJE, taught journalism and advised yearbook and newspaper for thirty-six years at the junior high and senior high levels. Both publications received Crown Awards from the Columbia Scholastic Press Association and Pacemaker Awards from the National Scholastic Press Association (NSPA). He is author of two textbooks—*Junior High Journalism* and *High School Journalism*—and author of NSPA's *Yearbook Guidebook* and coauthor of *Observe, React, Think, Write: A Novel Approach to Copy Writing*. He is past president of the Sponsors of School Publications of Greater St. Louis and of the Missouri Journalism Education Association and current president of the Journalism Education Association (JEA). He has been named JEA's Carl Towley Award winner and Yearbook Adviser of the Year, the Dow Jones Newspaper Fund's National Journalism Teacher of the Year, and NSPA's Pioneer Award winner. He is also a member of the National Journalism Hall of Fame and Missouri's Journalism Hall of Fame.

Richard P. Johns is executive director of Quill and Scroll Society (the international honorary society for high school journalists) at the University of Iowa School of Journalism and Mass Communication, as well as editor of *Quill & Scroll* magazine, published quarterly during the school year. He is also a member of the School of Journalism and Mass Communication faculty and teaches Advanced Media Design and Methods for Secondary School Journalism. His work in scholastic journalism has been recognized with the Columbia Scholastic Press Association's Gold Key; the Journalism Education Association's Carl Towley Award; and the National Scholastic Press Association's Pioneer Award. He teaches student editors and advisers at workshops and state high school press association conventions throughout the country.

Christine Kaldahl advises the newspaper, daily online newspaper, and yearbook and teaches mass media and beginning journalism at Millard South High School in Omaha, Nebraska. She earned her National Board Certification in Career and Technical Education in the 2001 cycle. She is among the first teachers in the country to certify in the area of journalism. Her bachelor's degree in journalism was earned at the University of Nebraska–Lincoln in 1991, and her master of arts degree in English was earned in 2001 from the University of Nebraska–Omaha. She has been teaching and advising in Nebraska for nine years.

Carol Lange, MJE, has taught for thirty years in Fairfax County, Virginia, in courses including English 9, 11, and 12, as well as photojournalism, and has advised twenty-six literary magazines and thirteen yearbooks. These publications have received the top awards of scholastic press associations and the National Council of Teachers of English. In 1991, the Dow Jones Newspaper Fund named her National High

School Journalism Teacher of the Year. She was a participant in the first ThinkQuest for Tomorrow's Teachers education Web site challenge. Her team received the platinum award in the content area category for its site "Only a Matter of Opinion?" Since July 1999, Lange has developed online curriculum for the Freedom Forum's First Amendment Center and the *Washington Post*. Lange has served as the secretary, newsletter editor, and state and regional director of the Journalism Education Association.

Eugenia Sarmiento Lotero was born in Bogotá, Colombia, and found her passion for teaching there. In 1986, as a Colombia pioneer in the Fulbright Exchange Program for Teachers, she taught in Denver, Colorado. After earning her Colorado teaching license, she taught for seven years at West High School in the Denver Public Schools. While there, she was nominated for the Disney Teaching Award. She earned her master's degree in Bilingual Multicultural Social Foundations from the University of Colorado at Boulder and was chosen as an American Council of Learning Societies Scholar. Now at Abraham Lincoln High School in Denver, she teaches Spanish for native speakers. During summers, she returns to Colombia, where she teaches a new approach to second-language acquisition.

Donna M. Spisso, CJE, has been teaching English for twenty-seven years, eight of them at Broadway High School, Virginia, and nineteen in American International Schools overseas in Madrid, Spain; Aruba (Netherlands Antilles); Leysin, Switzerland; Luxembourg, Grand Duchy of Luxembourg; Dhaka, Bangladesh; and, currently, Rome, Italy. She has advised the yearbook for fifteen years in international schools. Her staff's 1998 yearbook at American International School (AIS) of Dhaka was a combined book and CD package which won national recognition from the National Scholastic Press Association. Her most recent project at AIS Dhaka was to start a CNN Student Bureau. Her students produced a news feature on the Sundarbans mangrove forest, a World Heritage site, which was aired on CNN Newsroom on August 3, 2001.

*This book was typeset in Palatino and Helvetica by Electronic Imaging.
The typefaces used on the cover were Berling and Poetica Chancery.
The book was printed on 60-lb. Williamsburg Offset by Versa Press, Inc.*